BASICS FOR SCHOOL GOVERNORS

Joan Sallis

Network Educational Press Limited

The school curriculum changes, but unless the child has first mastered the Three Rs it will remain a mystery. Governors are no different. This best-selling book has been revised to take account of the new 'governors' curriculum' in the year 2000 and beyond, but the aim is still to help governors understand the unchanging basics - roles, relationships and rules.

Published by Network Educational Press Ltd
PO Box 635
Stafford
ST16 1BF

First Published 1993
Revised and updated 2000

ISBN 1 85539 012 4

Layout by Neil Hawkins
n.hawkins@appleonline of Devine Design

Printed in Great Britain by
Redwood Books, Trowbridge, Wiltshire

Contents

Part Two: Relationships

Understanding defensiveness... what can governors do to improve
relationships?... do some heads need to change?... perils of perfectionism...
valuing governors' skills.

Basics... building your own bridges... teacher governors... teachers and the
governing body... social events... when conflict is unavoidable...
thoughtfulness about teachers.

A new start for 'them and us'... the family grows up... support
in managing the school... working to the rules... maintaining good
relationships... accountability... what governors can do.

Part Three: Rules and Good Practices

Together ... openly... on a basis of equality... in short, democratically...
Are you a good team?

Meetings (notice, membership, chair, vice-chair, clerk)...making decisions...
headteacher...role of the chair... quorum... non-attendance... delegation...
committees...rescinding a resolution... co-options... removal of governors...
conflict of interest...visitors... general...Was it a good meeting?

Big events are not enough... neither is dropping in any time... every governing
body needs a system... practical advice on visiting... other ways of learning.

Valuing one another... looking ahead... sharing the work... avoiding A and B
teams... making space for colleagues... don't make a mystery of money...
organising major tasks... the role of the chair... If things go wrong it's because
you let it happen.

INTRODUCTION

Why you got involved
When you first became a school governor you must have been nervous. You had heard about what an important role it is now and about the work and responsibility. You wondered if you'd be out of your depth.

Yet you overcame your fear because you care a lot about education. If you are a parent governor, you'll feel a strong commitment to your local school and want to make it even better. You believe it is important that parents should have a voice. If you are a teacher, you think the school staff should have a say in how the school is run.

If you were appointed by a local authority or are a foundation governor of a church school, you see your school as part of something bigger - a service for children in the area, or a particular faith. You don't want it to become self-centred. And if you have been co-opted you will want to do your bit to keep school and neighbourhood in friendly contact.

When it gets hard
These are all good starting points. Yet often you will be overwhelmed by the paperwork, the unfamiliar words and procedures, the problems. You may feel isolated. Above all you will find it hard to sort out where the power lies, and how you get in there with your simple question, nagging worry or good idea. You desperately need somebody to remind you why you got involved in the first place, somebody to give you confidence to keep going. You may be drowning in information, but still asking some very basic questions.

Questions governors still ask

- *Why do schools have governors?*
- *What is my job, and where are the lines I mustn't cross?*
- *How can I get items discussed?*
- *Do I represent those who elected or appointed me, and if so do I consult them, speak for them, report back to them?*
- *How can I contribute at meetings when so much of what's decided seems all cut and dried?*
- *Are we all working to the same rules?*
- *If I think things aren't being done right is there anybody I can appeal to? Will I be seen as a trouble-maker?*

What this book tries to do

I assure you that these questions are asked by school governors everywhere. They need to know about the three Rs - **roles, relationships, rules.**

This book isn't a step-by-step guide to everything you have to know or do. If it were it would be a very long book and you wouldn't read it.

Nobody can take it all in at once anyway - all you want is to be able to find things out when you need them. My aim is to give you confidence that the job can be done and that it can be done by you, armed with a little basic understanding of your **role**, some guidance on how to cope with the **relationships**, and some knowledge of those **rules** which help governing bodies to better teamwork.

I hope to convince you that once you have solved these basic problems you will no longer feel that the job is too big for you or that you won't be able to get information when you need it. Everything is possible once a governing body is clear about its role, has sorted out its relationships with the professional staff of the school, and got its members working to the same rules. Such a governing body will operate fairly, openly and on a basis of trust and equality among its members. No powerful cliques. No need to be frightened that asking a question will label you a trouble-maker. No secret agendas. No A team and B team. Just one team - the school team.

PART ONE: ROLES

1 HOW AND WHY DID SCHOOLS COME TO HAVE GOVERNORS, AND HOW HAD THEIR ROLE EVOLVED BY THE END OF THE 20TH CENTURY?

Are governors a new idea?
Not at all. Schools have always had governors or something of the sort in this country. You may think they've only been in the news for a few years, and it's true that for long periods they haven't made much impact, but when Winchester College was founded over six hundred years ago a group of independent trustees were required to visit

> *with not more than six horses... to scrutinise the teaching and the progress in school of the scholars... and the quality of the food provided for the same... and correct or reform anything needing correction or reform.*

Four hundred years later the governors of a charity school (which still exists in London) visited weekly, made a termly formal inspection, supervised the tailoring of the grey school coats and doled out wool for the mothers to knit the school socks. So there's nothing new about governors keeping an eye on standards or getting involved in a practical way.

Remember, this started centuries before there were schools for all. Very few children received schooling, and what there was was privately funded. That makes it even more interesting that people thought some kind of public watch-dog was necessary. What was the thinking behind it?

Education concerns everybody...
People knew education was unique in its importance, not just to those in far-off days lucky enough to have it, but to everybody. Inside those schools were a few children who would one day have power and influence over others. There were also children who would grow up to have professional jobs, who would in their turn teach our children, heal our diseases, solemnise our marriages, write our wills - and children who would grow up to be writers, painters and musicians and give pleasure to others. What's more, schools influenced people's opinions and how they behaved with one another, so for many reasons it was important that there was some representation of the public. Our ancestors also thought that experts - like teachers - benefited from the influence of ordinary people, to keep their feet on the ground and their thinking in touch with everyday life. While teaching

itself was accepted as a highly skilled activity, the subjects taught and the ideas and beliefs put before children were considered to be a matter for society to debate and influence.

... especially when every child receives it and we all pay for it

In 1870 the first Education Act brought in elementary education for every child and provided for schools to be built and maintained from rates and taxes. That Act, and every one which followed, also provided for every school to have a body of local people to represent the public interest in its affairs. Much of the time in the hundred years or so between the 1870 Act and the changes of the 1980s there wasn't much life in the system, and in the memories of most of us school governors had become shadowy figures emerging now and then to present prizes or grant half holidays.

This was because early legislation and the 1944 Act had given governors very wide powers but didn't give much guidance about the sort of people they were to be. There were, of course, many conscientious governors who were devoted to their schools, but on the whole the system was moribund. Governors had little real involvement, and party political influence in their appointment was often excessive. In many areas during the 1970s parent and teacher governors were appointed, but usually only one token representative. In 1975 the government set up a committee under the chairmanship of Tom (now Lord) Taylor of Blackburn to review the whole system. Its recommendations became law in 1986.

School governing bodies today

The 1986 Education Act established school governors as a partnership of local education authority (LEA) (and in voluntary schools the church or other interests which originally provided the school), parents, teachers and, in county and controlled schools, co-opted representatives of the local community.
The tables in the Appendix show the composition of governing bodies as it had evolved by the year 2000. The changes implemented in 1999 increased parent representation, extended LEA representation, and provided a new category of support staff governor for all but the smallest schools. It also redefined governors' traditional role in sharper terms, emphasising their responsibility for school standards.

But the main features of the partnership had been established in 1986 as a whole-hearted response to the Taylor recommendations for a balanced membership and a real role, and we must begin our bird's-eye modern history there. The 1986 Act gave governing bodies, based on a partnership of the key stakeholders, clear responsibility for staff selection, curriculum policy and school spending, reviewing pupil exclusions, political and sex education and communication with parents. The Education Reform Act of 1988 added all the benefits of local management - budget planning and staff management, including appointments, gradings, pay, discipline and grievance procedures and dismissal. This Act also established a new type of state school called a grant-maintained school which could opt - following a ballot of parents - to receive its funds directly from the government, and enjoy the status of employer, decide its own admission procedures and have much of the freedom of a private company. It also had preferential funding, which, with the extended powers, tempted about 1000 schools to opt for the change. The School Standards and Framework Act of 1998 in effect partially re-integrated these schools into the LEA-maintained structure, on the one hand by giving all schools more freedom to manage themselves, and on the other by harmonising funding and admission systems and bringing LEA members onto their governing bodies. The schools concerned now have the choice of becoming foundation schools (which have to establish trustees and publish aims) or reverting to their former status. So much for the constitution of governing bodies and their general responsibilities at the start of the new Millennium.

But we now have to retrace our steps to the early 1990s to complete the record of the reorganisation which began in 1986-8. The Education Reform Act of 1988, as well as giving schools greater independence, created a more competitive market for education by ensuring that parental choice was not impeded by too many restrictions and would be backed up by published performance tables. This, it was believed, would raise standards. The standards agenda was moved further on in 1992 and 1993 by establishing regular OFSTED (Office for Standards in Education) inspections of all schools and provision for schools judged to be failing to be put on 'special measures' with a programme of directed improvement. Schools which, with support to achieve improvement, still failed to do so could be closed.

The implications of this clear agenda for school governors, who in many cases where schools were causing concern had either failed, or not been allowed to, exercise their proper functions, were serious, and increasingly the inspectors were briefed to investigate the role of governors in schools to identify cases where they needed more involvement.

The 1998 Education Framework and Standards Act of 1998 (substantially implemented in September 1999) not only changed the status and names of schools and the composition of their governing bodies, but also represented another major step in the drive for higher standards. It unambiguously laid upon governors the duty to conduct their schools in such a way as to improve performance. It empowered the Secretary of State to designate Education Action Zones where standards were generally low, and in these zones governors' powers in individual schools might have to be combined for the general good. It also introduced the inspection of whole LEAs which, if failing, might have their powers removed. It laid upon governors duties to write behaviour guidelines, set up home-school agreements and implement complaints procedures, and simultaneously the government moved ahead to require governors to set targets for school performance, reduce truancy, play a stronger role in exclusion cases, and gradually move into administering performance management pay for teachers.

This is a challenging agenda, and one with great potential for tension between governors and professionals. But in this book the aim is always to bring responsibilities down to simple principles, sound relationships and good working practices. These may not enable governors to solve all their problems, but one thing is certain: no problems can be solved without them. THUS...

In all types of school, it is important to emphasise:

(i) that governors have responsibility at policy-making level, not in the day-by-day running of the school, and

(ii) that power belongs to the governing body as a whole: the individual governor has no power to make decisions or take action.

Governors should always respect the skills and experience of teachers. But at the same time they should not assume that the skills and experience which they themselves bring to the task have less value. There is more to education than expertly finding the right way to teach a child to read or work with numbers, organising a classroom, knowing German or physics, being able to construct a timetable, plan an education activity or maintain order. You as a governor may not be able to do these things, but you are able to judge whether they are working and also whether the knowledge, skills and attitudes which are taught are what young people need when they go into the adult world. You are also able, by the decisions you make, to help create the most favourable conditions for learning to flourish - good use of money, a safe and pleasant environment, sound organisation, wise choice of staff, policies which are fair and which encourage good behaviour and motivate pupils and staff to do their best.

Because you live in the community and see the school as others see it you are also well placed to be a good ambassador for the school and a good messenger for the community - to explain, praise, defend, warn and guide.

The partnership between the governors and the school will work if both sides respect the skills and experience of the other, and especially if professionals accept that the perspective of ordinary people who care about education is just as important as their own. It will work if

governors are clear about their role and don't meddle in the day-by-day running of the school, but the other side of this is that professionals must accept governors' involvement at policy making level. If governors help to shape the policies they will not feel the need to meddle, and they will also be good ambassadors because they have a sense of ownership of those policies.

2   THE DIFFERENT KINDS OF SCHOOLS AND THEIR GOVERNORS

Many new governors are bewildered by the different ways schools, all within the state system, are described, and the different make-up of their governing bodies. Why do we only have one elected parent *(School A)* when my sister's school down the road which is no bigger has five *(School B)*? Why do we have no co-opted governors *(School C)*? Why does the school opposite have a representative of the parish council *(School D)*? Why does my friend's school have to fund-raise for repairs *(School E)*? She also says they are the employers of the staff and that they sometimes have assembly in the church. Why do we have five representatives of the LEA *(School F)* when the same size school on the far side of town *(School G)* only has one?

School A is a voluntary aided school. *School B* is a large community secondary school. *School C* is another voluntary aided school. *School D* may be a primary school where there is a minor local authority. *School E* is a voluntary aided school. *School F* is a large community or controlled school and *School G* will be a voluntary aided or foundation primary school. Yet all are state schools, if you define a state school as one whose running costs have traditionally come from public funds and where education is free to the user.

So what does it all mean? It doesn't seem quite so untidy if you know the history, but perhaps that's just because you've got used to it. So let us set out as simply as possible how it all began.

The early days of elementary education
There were schools in great variety from about a thousand years ago (see Chapter 1), but not many. These need not concern us here, since they educated only a tiny minority of children. The first schools to be provided on any scale were provided by voluntary bodies, mainly churches. Until 1833 these bodies provided the buildings and paid the teachers, but were finding it increasingly hard to meet the costs. Parliament in 1833 voted a sum of money to aid the voluntary bodies and these schools were the ancestors of our voluntary aided schools, though their number has greatly increased.

As the century wore on the church schools were nowhere near sufficient to meet the demands of an increasingly industrial and urban population. Employers wanted workers who could read and write and politicians were concerned that now that everybody had a vote there should be some basic education for all. The first Education Act, in 1870, provided for schools to be built from public funds to fill the gaps, and local 'school boards' were allowed to raise local rates to build and run elementary schools. These eventually became our county - now community - schools.

The Education Acts of 1902 and 1944 completed the integration of the voluntary schools into the state system (the UK is very unusual in having such integration: in most countries church schools are semi-private) and provided secondary as well as elementary education run by local education authorities. The arrangement with the voluntary bodies is, broadly speaking, that they own the buildings and have to keep the outside fabric in good repair and pay for any extensions or new buildings (they get a grant from the government towards these costs). The LEA pays the teachers and finances all the supplies and also pays for the inside of the building to be kept in good order. If additional land is needed the LEA provides it. Voluntary aided schools have the right to provide religious teaching of their own faith, have always employed the teachers, and have a say in what pupils they admit, usually giving some preference to their own church-goers.

Now in more detail...

Community schools
These used to be called county schools, wholly provided by local education authorities, who also own the land and buildings, are the employers of the staff (but from 1988 onwards not exercising the personnel functions of an employer), and decide which individual children get places. They have between two and five governors representing the LEA and between three and six elected representatives of parents. Religious education and worship are of a broadly Christian but undenominational character, and given in accordance with a local agreed syllabus into which other faiths established locally have an input.

Voluntary aided schools
These are the schools provided by voluntary bodies, mostly churches. Because of their history and the continuing responsibility for upkeep which they have accepted, the church has a more significant role, particularly in employment of staff, the admission of pupils and religious education. The church or other voluntary body also has an outright majority on the governing body, and this restricts the number of places given to parents and rules out co-options.

The foundation group must, however, while it has an overall majority, include two or three members who are also current parents. Interested people from the local community, including business, may well be appointed as foundation governors, but the choice is entirely for the voluntary body or bodies concerned.

Funds for building maintenance can come from the church, the diocese or a trust or be raised by the school, but like other state schools, aided schools provide free education and their rules for admitting pupils must conform to the law on parental preference and be made public. Apart from RE, the curriculum will be the same as in a county school.

Voluntary controlled schools

When consultations were going on about the 1944 Act it was clear that some voluntary schools were too poor to take on any financial responsibilities, though they still wanted to keep their distinctive character. These were allowed to choose controlled status. A controlled school has all its expenses paid by the LEA, but retains some say in religious education and the staff appointed to provide it. The foundation has some representation on the governing body (mostly at the expense of co-options) but in other ways a controlled school is much more like a county school, with parent and LEA governors according to size and a similar relationship with the local authority.

Special agreement schools

These are a group of over a hundred voluntary secondary schools established by agreement with LEAs in the 1930s. They need not concern us since to all intents and purposes they are treated as voluntary aided schools.

Grant-maintained schools *(a term now obsolete – see below.)*

These came into being as a result of the 1988 Act. If a ballot of parents provided a clear majority, schools could apply to the Secretary of State to opt out of LEA control and receive their funds directly from central government. Their governors had similar responsibilities. Former county schools and voluntary schools had five parent and one or two teacher governors but a majority over all other interests were appointed from the locality in former county schools and by the foundation in former voluntary schools.

Foundation schools

These came into being originally as grant-maintained schools, which under the 1988 Education Reform Act were able to opt out of LEA control and receive their funding direct from central government. In many respects foundation schools have greater independence to manage their own affairs than other state schools: they are the employers of the staff, and their governors decide whom to admit. The School Standards and Framework Act of 1998 brought them more into line again with other state schools, having their budget from the local authority once more, moving towards parity in funding and admission rules, and having LEA representation among their governors. As a result of this Act every such school had to establish a foundation with published aims but former grant-maintained schools also had the option of reverting to their pre 1988 status.

The Appendix shows the composition of governing bodies for the different types of school from September 1999.

3   THE ROLE OF THE GOVERNORS
IN THE SCHOOL

Representing the public

Schools are financed out of taxes - local and national - and the quality of the education they provide, the influence they have on their pupils and their smooth running are of concern to everybody. The governing body, working in partnership with the head and staff of the school, is the agency through which the school is accountable to the local authority and to its community, both for its use of public funds and its effectiveness. It is also there to ensure good relationships between the school and the community it serves. It brings together a number of interests - the local education authority and, in the case of voluntary schools, the church or other body which provided the school, the parents, the teachers and the community. The head teacher may be a governor if s/he wishes.

Responsibility

The governing body is responsible for how the school uses its money, for the character of its individual curriculum and organisation and the choice of its staff. Even if it chooses to delegate some tasks which can legally be delegated, to the head or its own members, the governing body as a whole remains responsible. It is also responsible for ensuring that the school gives parents the information they are entitled to by law, and for ensuring fairness to individual pupils and staff in certain kinds of dispute.

Boundaries

Distinctions have often been made between 'governance' and 'management' to provide a demarcation between governors' responsibilities and those of professionals. In a setting wherein governors decide the distribution of the budget, are responsible overall for academic standards, care of the premises, staff appointments and dismissals, personnel and pupil discipline policies, communication and marketing, one can no longer draw this distinction. It must be accepted that governors share in every aspect of the strategic management of the school. Note that word 'strategic', for it is the key to maintenance of workable boundaries.

Nor is it possible to draw lines like fences between one activity and another: the lines dividing professionals and governors are horizontal, dividing the same activity into layers representing strategic and operational levels like floors in a high building. Thus governors ultimately decide whether the school continues to offer Latin as an option despite a small uptake, but teachers decide on which Latin textbook to

use. Governors decide on appropriate systems of reward and punishment, but teachers decide whether to give David a merit or Ann a detention. Governors decide whether to move from mixed ability to setting, but teachers decide how to categorise the pupils. A multi-storey building is a good illustration, because people do go up and down the stairs to talk to each other and observe how things are working out. Otherwise those who operated the systems would do so without understanding or reflection, and those who established systems would be fanciful and unrealistic.

Specifics
Governors' territory for decision-making covers all aspects of school activity:

- **Curriculum** The latest legislation makes governors responsible for so conducting the school as to improve its standards of performance. This means ensuring the delivery of the national curriculum, with special attention to RE and worship, special needs, political and sex education and citizenship, and it involves target-setting and monitoring.

- **Budget** Governors decide on the use of funds to meet the school's needs, normally with the school having flexibility to move specified maximum amounts from one budget head to another if need be.

- **Staffing** Governors choose head and deputy and have such involvement in other appointments as they consider necessary to give effect to their responsibility. The governing body decides on the staffing structure and the gradings of teachers within it. It is responsible for discipline and grievance procedures and dismissal, and for determining pay levels within the national scales.

- **Premises** Governors ensure that the premises are safe and healthy and provide a stimulating learning environment. They also decide on the use of premises outside school hours and (after consultation with parents if there are to be changes) opening and closing times for the school.

- **Discipline** Governors prepare guidelines to ensure good behaviour. They also review more serious pupil exclusions and decide whether to confirm the punishment.

- **Communication** Governors see that parents get all the information they are legally entitled to both about their own children and the school policies. They draw up home/school agreements on mutual obligations with parents and (from the year 2000 to 2001) complaints procedures. They draw up an annual report to parents and arrange a meeting to discuss it.

- **Inspection** Following an OFSTED inspection governors draw up an action plan to respond to the inspectors' findings, and monitor its achievement.

- **Major changes in the character of the school** Governors must be consulted about any major changes in the status and character of the school.

These are headline responsibilities. But they show the range and importance of governors' involvement in every aspect of school life.

Drawing the line

Governors are for the most part people with jobs of their own and they are not educationists. Teachers have had a long training and are experienced as well as skilled in helping children to learn. Headteachers and other senior staff have come to the top of their profession by reason of their expertise as educationists and their ability to manage the learning programme of a school and direct and guide the people taking part in it. Increasingly heads also need management skills of a high order, since schools are complex organisations using large and varied resources.

Head and staff work full-time in the school and no governor could match the detailed knowledge this involves. It is not realistic, nor would it be right, for governors to imagine that they could replace a professional in making day-by-day decisions about teaching techniques or the management of time, space, equipment and staff within the school. This is not their role.

Am I just there to support the school?

Governors often say their main job is to support the school. Heads often say, 'My governors are so supportive'. But the governors play many parts.

Of course governors are supporters. They are also at different times ambassadors and interpreters and often critical friends. All these roles they can have informally as individuals. But when it comes to the serious parts they play - monitoring, judging, mediating, warning, even sometimes requiring something to be changed - remember that it isn't the individual governor who has these roles. These are the tasks of the governing body, working together within fairly strict rules, and if necessary by majority vote. Individual governors cannot, on their own authority, inspect, reward, arbitrate, discipline, suspend, dismiss, authorise spending or lay down policies. It is vital that governors understand this. It is also important that teachers understand it, because it takes the fear out of the relationship. If a governor comes into school, it is to learn, not to judge.

13

When heads say that their governors are supportive, they may mean that because the governors have a genuine policy-making role they will naturally support the outcomes. Often, however, they mean that professional decisions are accepted without question and governors don't interfere. Uncritical support isn't worth very much. It's also quite dangerous to make too many decisions alone. Shared decisions are stronger. With the pressures on schools today and the criticism they often attract from outside, as well as with so much power now being delegated to schools, a head who doesn't share is very exposed.

What makes a good governor?

It would be a pity if any keen and committed person was driven away by mistaken notions about governors having to have special skills or knowledge. The history of the school governor is all about the belief which people have had for centuries that education is not just a matter for the educators, and that the precious light of ordinariness must be allowed to shine on expert activities if those activities are to be healthy. So the first qualification must be ordinariness. Everybody has skills - listening, peace-making, organising, throwing ideas into the air, catching ideas and patiently working them through. A good governing body will have a mix of these skills, and schools must make it clear that they're not just looking for accountants and lawyers.

The main requirements are:

- **Interest in education and commitment to that school**
- **Tolerance and ability to work with others**
- **Patience: everything takes a long time**
- **Enthusiasm**
- **Willingness to learn**
- **Willingness to spend what time you have getting involved in the school**
- **A strong feeling about doing things openly and democratically.**

Confidence in your role

It is indeed a responsible job and you can't help feeling nervous. Remember, however, that you have been appointed, elected or co-opted by people who had confidence that you could do the job. Remember too that the whole idea of governors rests on the fact that they are ordinary people from the local community served by the school, bringing everyday experience to the task. Remember that although it is a heavy responsibility, it isn't one you bear alone but only as a member of a team. Finally, be assured that you will never as a governing body have to make any decision without expert advice if you want it. There is expertise of all kinds available to governors as well as training and support. You are there not because you are an expert, but because you are not. You will of course be eager to learn and will work hard at becoming better informed. Information and practice will bring confidence. But the object is not to change you into an education expert, and the confidence must be in the fresh perspective you bring to bear on the work of experts and your ability to work in partnership with them.

REPRESENTING OTHERS

I have already said that school governing bodies represent the public interest in schools and that they must work in unity. But individual governors are appointed by the LEA or foundation, elected by parents or teachers, or co-opted from the local community. Each group brings a different viewpoint and represents a different interest, and this section aims to explain how to do your duty by those you represent and still keep the unity of the governing body.

The starting point is that the first loyalty of every governor must be to the governing body. The interests of a particular group - parents, staff, the local residents' association, a political party - must never be allowed to divide governors from one another in their primary duty to the school and their commitment to majority decisions.

But each governor does, nevertheless, represent a particular interest, an important point of view. He or she must present it clearly and may even argue it strongly. It is after all intended that the governing body takes account of all interests and that is why it brings together representatives of several groups.

In the end, however, having made sure that they have fairly conveyed to their colleagues the views of those they represent, governors listen to all the arguments, weigh them up and come to a conclusion based on the interest of the school as they see it and in the light of all the information. This may be the same as the group they represent or it may be in conflict. Then, when a decision is democratically arrived at, every governor must stand by it.

Governors may have been told that they do not 'represent' parents, teachers, the police, the district council, local business, and so on, but that they serve solely in an individual capacity. Sometimes this arises from genuine confusion or misunderstanding. Often it is a very proper attempt to convey that the first duty is to the school. Sometimes it arises from a fear, conscious or unconscious, that if governors put forward strong points of view which are backed by a powerful group, it may rock the boat.

It is important to get this right. The real problem is confusion between being a delegate and being a representative. A delegate is there to obey instructions from an interest group and vote on every issue as instructed. Governors are not delegates. A representative, on the other hand, is not obliged to vote in accordance with instructions, but is obliged, if he or she has been elected or appointed by a group (as distinct from being chosen as an individual), to listen, to carry views and concerns to the governing body and to report back. Once this is clear the role of a governor day-by-day becomes a lot easier. In the pages which follow examples are given to clarify the difference between the delegate and the representative roles.

LEA governors

LEA governors are appointed by the Education Committee of the local council. In some areas this is a strictly political activity, with places being allocated in proportion to the strength of the parties on the council. In other areas there is no political test, and appointments are made on the basis of the individual's interest and experience.

If LEA governors represent a particular party they clearly have a point of view to express. They will not be popular on most governing bodies today if they push too hard: rightly or wrongly most governors feel that party politics are out of place in school affairs.

It is reasonable that any LEA governor sees the school's decisions in the setting of a local service meeting children's needs. This may be a broader view than that of a parent or teacher governor. There may well be conflict when, for instance, some reorganisation or economy is proposed which the school doesn't welcome. The LEA governor is there to put forward this broader view. In the end, however, when all opinions have been heard, the LEA governor may be convinced that the school's interests over-ride the general considerations and is not then obliged to vote on the party line.

Foundation governors

In church schools (or schools established by other voluntary bodies), or foundation schools, these governors are appointed to represent the interests of those who originally provided the school. Foundation governors have a particular responsibility to see that the school is run in accordance with the beliefs of the founding organisation. In many cases there is a trust deed which lays down certain principles which must be followed, and these should be observed not just by foundation governors but by all governors of such a school. In making appointments, for instance, there might be conflict if the trust deed of a Roman Catholic school said that the school must observe a faith which upholds the sanctity and permanence of marriage, and some governors wished exceptionally to appoint a divorced person to a senior post.

Parent governors

Parent governors are elected by the parents of the school, They are not delegates and do not have to vote as instructed by parents. On the other hand, the fact of being elected gives parent governors a representative role, and they are right to feel that they must use every opportunity to find out parents' views, to listen to their concerns, and to carry those concerns if they are of a general character to the governing body. They also have a duty to report back as best they can to the parent body.

How well parent governors manage to listen and report back will depend a great deal on the type of school (it tends to be easier in primary than secondary schools, since the latter serve a wider area, parents don't normally gather at the gate, and the whole set-up is more formal and complex). It also depends on how open a school it is and how well it communicates with parents itself. In general, parent governors should attend as many parent gatherings as possible and keep in close touch with the parents' association. In some schools the current parent governors are automatically members of the parents' association committee. In others, they have a slot in the parents' association or school newsletter for governors' business, or a chance to report at parents' association meetings. Some schools even give parent governors a chance to use the school child-post to communicate with parents as necessary, with tear-off slips for return of views.

Parent governors are correct to see their role in terms of bringing general parent concerns to the governing body, though they must propose items for the agenda in the normal way if they don't naturally arise from items being discussed and they should never, except in an emergency, raise them without warning. As already stated, they can report parent views without being in agreement themselves. For example, parents might support a familiar graded reading scheme which was in use when they were children. The parent governors might report this view, but might themselves have been totally convinced by professional arguments for a more modern scheme or a more flexible combination of techniques to teach reading. In this case the parent governors should do all they can to reassure parents and put the case for what has been decided by the governing body. Parents in a secondary school might find it hard to accept moving away from separate sciences - physics, biology and chemistry - and governors who had been convinced otherwise might need to produce arguments that broad and balanced science was not a 'dilution' and prepared students adequately for A levels and a career in science. Many parents might favour a strict school uniform, while governors might have been convinced by professional arguments to the contrary. These are very common conflicts. In all cases, however, governors must make sure that they do report parents' views and listen carefully and critically to the arguments so that they themselves are not persuaded against their better judgement.

One problem which often bothers parent governors is what to do about individual concerns brought to them by parents. They don't always know what to do with them. They may sense that the headteacher doesn't like parents to go direct to governors in this way.

Headteachers should be realistic about this issue. Obviously parents should ideally bring concerns to the class or subject teacher - questions like whether a child should be on a higher reading book, whether a child with eczema can bring his or her own soap, how to deal with a fear or phobia. But many parents will always be fearful of schools, however open they are, and will see closed doors where there are none. They will be afraid that their concerns are 'too trivial' or that they've got the wrong end of the stick and will look foolish. It's a lot easier to ask somebody you know in the supermarket or the library or at the gate, especially as you can do that without thinking about it too long beforehand and getting nervous. After all, the important thing is that the worry gets brought out and dealt with, not by what route.

A parent governor should try to get parents with a worry to go direct to the teacher or head. If they are timid s/he should go with them. If they are very timid s/he should go for them. Individual worries should not be brought up at governors' meetings unless they reveal a general concern which might need a rule or policy to be discussed. Even in this case the head should always be approached first and should not be bypassed. Head teachers for their part should try to be more relaxed about communication which doesn't come directly to them. It is quite natural to feel threatened by it, but it is also natural that parent governors get approached by less confident parents. It is far better that these concerns get dealt with than that they are suppressed. Sometimes an experienced parent governor can helpfully discuss with the head how arrangements for parents to bring concerns to the school could be improved or publicised more successfully.

Teacher governors
Teacher governors have, in some ways, the most difficult role on the governing body. They are discussing the affairs of the school frankly in the presence of 'outsiders' and their head teacher, who has a big influence on their career prospects. They may also feel conflicts of loyalty. A wise head will make it clear to teacher governors that s/he welcomes open debate and will not let it affect his or her opinion of the teacher or the latter's career. Such a head will encourage teacher governors to play a confident part.

Teacher governors are elected by their colleagues and this gives them a representative role. They are not delegates - i.e. they do not necessarily have to act in accordance with the views of the other teachers - but they must give colleagues a chance to express those views (by showing them the agenda and explaining issues to them) and they must also report back decisions on matters which have not been classified by the governing body as confidential. Minutes and other governors' papers should be available in the staff room.

Supposing governors were to discuss imposing a smoking ban in the staff room, and just supposing (though it's unlikely) that the teacher governors were the only non-smokers. Their colleagues might well urge them to vote against the ban. If they were delegates they would have to do so. But their representative role involves listening to and carefully reporting the staff's views. If then they have been convinced by other arguments, by what they have heard about the effects of 'passive' smoking, by the fact that some children as young as nine start smoking by copying others and their consciences dictate voting for the ban, they should do so. They would then have to report to colleagues why they made the decision.

Supposing the requirements of the national curriculum led governors to consider extending the school day to finish at 4.00 pm instead of 3.30 pm. This would of course have to go to parents for final approval, but the governors' views are crucial. Staff who live near might accept easily, but in this area where property is expensive imagine a majority had a long journey by road. They might say that they would already be into rush-hour traffic before they reach home and the journey would be longer and more stressful. Teacher governors would carefully report these considerations to governors. On the other hand, the teacher governors would have taken part in all the discussion about the national curriculum requirements and would have accepted that children were losing out if teaching time could not be extended. They would rightly see themselves as part of group which is concerned for the school and this over-rides their view as individuals. So they might vote for the 4 o'clock change, or they might suggest starting 15 minutes earlier instead and taking another 15 minutes off the lunch hour.

A special problem with teacher governors is that sometimes they are discouraged or even prevented from playing a full part in governing body duties. Their fellow governors or the head may, for instance, not be happy about their representing the governors in selecting senior staff. They may be told that it isn't appropriate for them to be on committees which are concerned with pay, redundancy, or other personnel issues.

The law intends all governors to play as full a part as possible in the work of the governing body. There is no general restriction on teacher governors being chosen for staff selection panels or being on committees which are concerned with staff matters, but since September 1999 they have been barred from participation in discussion of the pay or appraisal of an individual colleague. In fact it is particularly important that a teacher governor should be on the finance committee and other committees of concern to staff if only to reassure colleagues of the fairness of decisions. Subject to the one qualification already mentioned, teacher governors are only prevented from carrying out these duties if they have an interest 'greater than the generality of teachers' in the outcome. This means that they can take part as long as they don't stand to gain personally from the decision; e.g. step into a vacancy created by an appointment, benefit uniquely from a pay policy, or influence the decision about an excluded pupil where they were directly involved in the incident leading to the exclusion. Rules about personal interest apply to all governors.

It may be argued that some issues concerning staff are too delicate or embarrassing for teacher governors to participate in. That is for them to decide: they can always decline to be involved in something they find too painful. The object of the rules is simply to exclude from decisions people who might be thought to be biased, not to save people embarrassment. And, as stated elsewhere, it is an important principle that governors are equally trusted with the difficult and sometimes delicate tasks they share.

Support staff governors
Since September 1999 almost all schools have to include an elected representative of the non-teaching staff on the governing body. This reform is long over-due, since support staff are an essential part of the whole school team and often have very distinctive perspectives. It is important that they are welcomed by colleagues and treated as equals in every way - it is necessary to say this because some of the new governors may have hard and lowly-paid jobs and may not feel as much at home on a committee as some other groups. Having said that, the category covers all those who work full time or part-time on a regular basis in the school, and they will range from cleaners to bursars. But even so, any new group will tend to lack confidence. It must be stressed that they are in every sense full governors (apart from a few legal restrictions on all governors who work in the school e.g. they can't be chair and they can't take part in a discussion of the pay or appraisal of an individual.) They are entitled to play a full part as governors and enjoy our unqualified trust.

This group will have particular problems arising from the variety of staff they represent, the different hours those staff work and areas of the school they work in. It will be specially important for their governor to communicate with them all and this will need more organising than teachers, for instance, need. There may often also be tricky conflicts between the interests of different groups, and the governor will have to be scrupulously fair to all, always remembering that in the end s/he is not a delegate, and that when an issue has been thoroughly discussed and all the different points of view aired, the interests of the school and its pupils are paramount for any governor.

Co-opted governors

In community schools these are the largest group. They represent a wide variety of interests and bring different skills and experience to the governing body. Their accountability is clearly not as precise as that of elected parent or teacher governors because their 'constituency' can't easily be identified.

But they bring a perspective from outside the school and outside the education service, and should be particularly watchful for the school's relationship with the community.

Co-opted governors may come from business - governors are advised to have regard to this interest. They may come from a residents' association or other community group, or from agencies concerned with children's welfare, or from schools/colleges which feed or follow on from the school in question. They may be parents who have served in that capacity and retained a more general interest in the school even though their families have left. They are all well-placed to see the school as its neighbours see it, and even though all governors should be concerned about community links, co-opted governors can often be more objective about this.

Things to watch for are that the school is considerate to its neighbours - in the behaviour of its pupils, noise and litter, road and transport use; that it is generous and imaginative in sharing its facilities; that it uses the environment and the skills of local people to enrich the experience of pupils; and that it listens and communicates well about school policies.

Confidentiality

All school governors are concerned about confidentiality. Since anyone can come in from the street and ask to see governors' agendas, papers and minutes, it follows that the law intends that in general governors' business should be open. Items exceptionally classified as confidential are excluded from published papers. Any visitors are asked to leave when such items are discussed. So what items are confidential and who decides?

The governing body decides whether an item should be classified as confidential. It isn't a matter for the LEA or the chair, the head or the clerk. If governors don't specifically rule an item confidential, it isn't. It is clear that the law intends confidentiality to be kept to a minimum, mainly used for items affecting the privacy of an individual. In reporting back to the group they represent on non-confidential items, however, governors should confine themselves to the outcomes and perhaps, where appropriate, the main arguments on each side. They should avoid reporting who said what, how individuals voted and other personal details which offend against the unity of the governing body. They must also remain loyal to the decision, even if they were personally against it.

5   REAL INVOLVEMENT IN DECISIONS

Governors are intended to be initiators, collaborators or, at the very least, actively consenting partners in all important school decisions - on the school's development plan, curriculum policy, finance, organisation, staff structure and staff selection. They are also intended to have agreed policies on discipline, sex education, religious education and worship, charging for school activities and staff pay.

This does not mean that governors order the green maths book to be used on Wednesday in Year 9, sign a slip authorising the payment of the gas bill, supervise the move of an over-large class into a bigger classroom previously occupied by a smaller class, or tell Mrs Willing to keep an eye on Class 3 as well as her own while their teacher talks to the LEA inspector for primary education about the SATs arrangements. These are day-by-day management issues. It would be different if the head of maths was proposing to give up using the green maths book and go over to an entirely new system of teaching maths using only sundials, kitchen scales and puzzles from the Sunday Times. It might be different if the school's use of gas so exceeded estimates that they needed to use a very large sum from another budget head to fill the gap, or even decided not to fill a teaching post for the time being. It would be different if, because of unevenly sized classes, the school proposed going over to mixed age grouping throughout. It would be different if it came up as a policy issue that not just Mrs Willing but any Class 4 teacher should be paid an extra allowance for the constant added responsibility of covering for the SATs class.

The right level and the right timing
These frivolous examples illustrate the *level* at which governors should expect to be involved. The *timing* is the other important factor, since even if governors are brought in at the right level, it isn't satisfactory if they are only used to sanction actions which have already taken place. Many governors complain that their meetings are nothing but rubber-stamping exercises, that they are not expected to question anything and it would be too late anyway.

Governors who have discussed a school's new policy on teaching reading have understood as a result of explanations from the teaching staff exactly how they approach the task, the implications of moving to a different scheme, how that scheme has worked in other schools and in trial runs, are most unlikely to criticise a reading lesson on a visit to the school. Governors who have, after discussion with staff, laid down principles on pupil behaviour and on punishments are less likely to disagree with the

**action taken when a pupil misbehaves. They are also more likely to
understand that it is the governing body which is entitled to comment, not
the individual visiting governor. But heads and staff must play the game
if governors confine themselves to policy matters. They must abide by
those policy decisions. If governors have said in their finance committee
that expenditure on teaching staff must be maintained at all costs, it isn't
the head's role to decide not to advertise a vacant post because he's
worried about the gas bill. If governors in their discipline policy (in
consultation with staff, of course) have said that no punishment should be
humiliating, they have a right to comment if a boy is made to wear girls'
clothing all day for peeping in the girls' toilets.**

Should governors take the initiative?

A governing body which takes an exaggerated view of its role might be on
constant look-out for changes to propose and possible innovation in the school.
This isn't a good approach at all. We are not educationists and most of the time
we can assume that teachers have thought carefully about how the school is run,
that from time to time they will themselves suggest some change which they think
would improve it and submit that idea for governors' comments. In other words,
it is realistic to expect that mostly when governors consider possible
developments or changes it will be as a result of professional initiatives. But
there are three points to make:

- One is that governors as outsiders can sometimes see things that experts
  miss and that from time to time they will have brainwaves or notice
  something that's not working well.
- Secondly, if suggested changes are brought to governors it should be at a
  stage when there's time for consultation, not when everything's cut and
  dried.
- Thirdly, a governing body which is working well should be engaged in
  planning for the school and methodically reviewing different aspects of
  its work, in consultation with staff, all the time. It is not there simply to
  react.

How should the school be managing governors' involvement in decisions?

Firstly, it is necessary for head and senior staff to accept that this must happen.
Traditional ways of decision-making must change, and senior management in
schools must plan for collaborative policy-making. If governors' involvement is
not to be too late (or too early - time can be wasted on things staff haven't been
sounded out on), then governor-talk and teacher-talk must be woven together
more, to achieve understanding of issues. There must be some governors in staff
meetings and more teachers on governors' committees and working parties. The

time-scale must be watched carefully in relation to governors' meeting dates and collecting and preparing information to help them look at issues. Professionals mustn't be too perfectionist - it's a good professional characteristic normally to want a paper to be as good as you can make it before you go public, but something that seems finished and perfect doesn't encourage polite governors to comment. Consulting at sketch-plan stage, asking questions to which you may not know the answers, thinking aloud, may not come naturally to a teacher, but it makes for better collaboration. Infallibility makes admirers, but few friends.

What can governors do to ensure that their involvement is real?
There is one sure way to improve matters and that is to look ahead. If a governing body never thinks beyond the meeting agenda it is almost certain that it will spend most of its time looking at things which have already happened. Head teachers should be encouraged to begin each meeting (especially the first of the school year) giving a brief account of the issues which they expect to be most important in the period before the next meeting, or governors may like to ask for the head's report routinely to include a look into the near future in this way. The governors can plan how they are going to organise themselves to consider these issues, which may mean changing meeting dates, fixing extra meetings or setting up small groups to do preliminary work. Above all, this good habit will in time focus minds within the school on the governors' role and the need to plan for more collaborative decision-making. Much of the time nobody deliberately sets out to make governors an afterthought: it is simply that established routines are hard to change, and a rigid pattern of governor involvement, which looks backwards rather than forwards, is a relic of the past. It is also helpful if a few interested governors participate at the brain-storming stage when teachers are beginning to change a policy or practice: they may be better able to contribute ideas than comment on a final polished paper. Schools traditionally do their thinking 'in turns'. We must move to thinking 'in step'.

The process of regularly reviewing all aspects of the school's life and work also helps governors and teachers together to focus on the future. If a governing body has a curriculum working party, teachers could be invited in turn to talk about their departments, development plans and their future needs. The whole governing body can also invite teachers in turn to attend and talk to governors. This builds relationships and helps teachers 'de-mystify' governors and see them as people who can help provide the support for their particular plans and hopes.

Part Two: RELATIONSHIPS

6 RELATIONSHIPS BETWEEN GOVERNORS
AND HEAD TEACHER

Most jobs can be done a lot better when the relationships are good. But the job of school governors can hardly be done at all without good relationships: with the LEA, the head and staff of the school, and one another. Unquestionably the most important of these relationships is that between the governors and the head.

Mutual respect, a proper sharing of important decisions, trust, humour and flexibility would be on many people's list for a good marriage, and it's the same with governors and head. In addition, it's vital that each should accept the other's contribution as of equal value and recognise that both have the same objectives.

There will inevitably be misunderstanding and clumsiness, but these should be small matters between people whose concerns are the same: children have enough enemies in the world without natural allies falling out. If this is accepted, the occasional lapse can be shrugged off or laughed at rather than taken as the end of a beautiful friendship.

There will be lapses. This is partly because one is dealing with the involvement of non-professionals in what has always been largely professional territory, so that the new participants will sometimes tread on corns without even knowing they are there. It is also because the territorial lines often have to be negotiated on the spot - there are few policemen around to settle boundary disputes. We are talking about sharing power, and sharing hurts. Only the acceptance that sharing is (a) right, (b) likely to produce a better result and (c) good for relationships makes the hurt worthwhile.

Understanding why professionals are sometimes defensive
Governors do frequently complain that they find teachers and heads very touchy about territory. They don't understand, governors say to me, that I don't want to run the school. I wouldn't know how to run a school, I haven't got time to run a school. Yet when I ask an innocent question, they say, because I'm nervous and I may have waited a long time to ask, it somehow comes out all wrong and aggressive and gets taken the wrong way. The unseen curtains come down, they say. Why can't my goodwill be taken for granted?

One answer has already been given. Sharing power is painful. Also some people feel very threatened by it. On the whole the most confident manage it better. But there are other reasons too. Many people in education are very stressed as a result of so much change coming in so fast. Schools are under great pressure, and often feel that they are the victims of unfair public criticism as well. Isn't it always when you feel tired and stressed even in the home that you try to do everything yourself, snatch jobs away from people, assume nothing can happen if you aren't around?

Secondly, many heads have had bad experiences of governors in the past. In the old days some governors often had little real personal commitment to the school. They were there because they had been pushed into it by their political party, or to have something good to put on their job application, or just for the ego-trip. Our GP once said to me after a hard birth, 'You know my job is to produce live babies not to give you a beautiful experience.' We have to convince professionals that we are there for the sake of the live babies, not seeking a beautiful experience. There's nobody else to convince them.

We also have to convince professionals that we care about all the children in the school, especially those who find life hard. Some teachers - the best - are passionately protective towards those children who don't have confident adults to participate on their behalf, and they fear, quite wrongly often, that we represent the privileged and might even draw time and resources away from the needy. Only we can prove we are not like that.

Finally, there is the fear that governors who may be uninformed about education or even have some old-fashioned ideas about it, going back to their own schooldays, will see themselves as inspectors and come into school criticising everything, upsetting teachers, laying down the law. We'll remember that it's the governing body that has the power and that we as individuals are not inspectors. We'll also remember that even if governors have a critical role sometimes, the best basis for starting a relationship is shared enthusiasm, so we'll find out what the school is most proud of and identify those responsible, see how they do it, remember to praise and encourage.

What else can governors do to improve relationships?
Needless to say, you'll show interest in the school and willingness to learn. Without undervaluing the fresh and valuable perspective which you as an outsider bring to it, you will also respect the professional skills of teachers and encourage them to demonstrate them to you by talking about their work and setting out the educational arguments on every issue.

You will also show willingness to help the school in practical ways. I'm not suggesting that governors should get stuck into decorating classrooms or mending books, but there is a tendency among heads to divide parents and other interested adults into good sorts (who are in the Parents or Friends Association) and stirrers (who tend to be on the governing body!) For all our sakes these lines ought to be blurred, a bit more stirring from the Parents Association and the acceptance that governors are good sorts too. I've found in all my activities that willingness to do something useful and uncontroversial is always an asset when you do need to be a little more awkward. Anyway, helping as an extra pair of hands on an outing, or giving out the lemonade when they come back from the sponsored walk, is a learning experience too.

Here are some tips you may not have thought of:

- **Remember to congratulate teachers who have done something special - carried through a curriculum innovation, taken an extra qualification, run some outstanding out-of-school activity.**
- **Find out a bit about teachers' working conditions and amenities - they are often shocking and wouldn't be accepted in business. Show concern and persist in trying to get improvements.**
- **Think whether, through your work or connections or your own skills, there is any resource that you could offer the school.**
- **Where possible find a positive starting point for seeking information or questioning a policy - 'I was so pleased to have those details of staff development activities in the report. Do we have any training for non-teaching staff?' Or 'It was extraordinary to have over half the age group with A to C grades in science especially when it's a new course. The teaching is clearly superb. But there were hardly any Ds or Es. Are we encouraging too many to take the alternative non-examination course?'**
- **Ask necessary questions, but don't get into a habit of asking for information for the sake of it or just to show you're awake. Have a clear idea what use you will make of it. Remember it takes time and that time could be used with the pupils.**
- **It's sometimes wise to give someone else the credit - or not complain if they take it - for your good idea. After all, what matters is that the right thing is done for the pupils, not who gets the glory.**

Do some heads need to change?

Relationships would be transformed if all heads were equally convinced

(a)   that governors' new role is here to stay;

(b)   that it represents a legitimate public concern and right; and

(c)   that the positive benefits in terms of good ambassadors for schools, more public understanding of the needs of schools, a better image for state education and more priority in resources, could be enormous.

Many do have this vision of what could be, and are working at the admittedly difficult task of managing schools in a genuinely collaborative way. Some of us may be in a position to help convince the others. Also, most heads are governors of their schools and so may be reading this.

What most needs to change is how governors are seen in the management process. Too often informing and involving governors is seen as a separate activity, and governors are seen as a group, good or bad, beyond further development - strange in a service which is all about human development - whom schools did not choose. Thus a head teacher will say in private that the governors are awful but would be ashamed to say that of staff because developing staff and using them well is a prime management task. Or s/he will say they are wonderful, or, like a Victorian wife, that they 'don't trouble me often'. Neither way is it seen as a test of leadership.

If there is one thing we can do to move things on, it is to convince our heads that the finest flowering of managerial talent is in the development of a governing body as a well-informed, highly motivated and sharing team.

The perils of perfectionism

Good professionals are perfectionists. We all benefit from that. They also feel the need to be a step ahead. We benefit from that too, mostly - under the surgeon's knife, for instance, or when the plumber remembers to turn the water off first. There are times, however, when teachers' desire not to go public on anything until it's as good as they can make it keeps the governors in the rubber-stamping business. Nice people don't like to question a document which looks so finished and shiny. Also the desire to have a first look at an incoming circular to make sure you understand it yourself before you discuss it with anybody means that many head teachers have unopened brown envelopes downstairs in their homes while they toss and turn sleepless above. Stress isn't caused by the work you do but by the work you haven't even opened. Stress is an unopened brown envelope.

Discussion of school proposals at sketch-plan stage must be encouraged. So must sharing of brown envelopes straight from the post. See what is said in Chapter 12 about spreading the workload.

Valuing and using governors' skills
I once said to a highly qualified educationist that there were a few quite exceptionally able people on the Taylor Committee (the Committee which in the 70s recommended all these changes in the governing bodies and on which I served as a parent). Really, she said, such as? I mentioned about four for a start. But, she said, surely they haven't got MAs? (I think some of them may have, but it's a matter of pride not to admit it, like surgeons being called Mister.) I'm not suggesting there are many people around who take such a limited view of human skills, but we all have a tendency to over value the ones we know about.

On a governing body there will be an amazing collection of skills. Sometimes they are never discovered. A good head will discover them, respect them, use them. There isn't just one kind of ability either. Every governor can help make this point in different ways and set a good example. Draw attention to colleagues' strong points. Then perhaps the professionals will notice too.

7   BEST FRIENDS WITH TEACHERS

Teachers feel these days that they don't have many best friends. You know that. Perhaps you don't know, however, what fear some of them feel about governors. In their experience there is often a gap between the school governors of their childhood, shadowy figures emerging now and then for some ritual but not really anything to do with children and teachers, and the monsters of their newspapers, asking outrageous questions at interviews and then having the power of life and death over them. In between dwell the real governors of the new Millennium. In between also dwell fear and suspicion.

Basics
If you are very lucky, you may have a head who has tried to fill this gap with reality. That head will have acquainted teachers with the inevitability of amateur interference (as some teachers see it) in education, and pointed out that all important decisions in society are made, not by experts, but by representative people of some kind. Also that in relationships with other professionals, there is some debate about objectives and outcomes and some communication about methods, the loss of which in education is responsible for some of the poor publicity education receives.

That wise head will also have said that individual governors have no power and come into school only to learn: it is only the governing body which has power. S/he will have encouraged teachers to share some of their enthusiasms and problems with governors, to welcome them into classrooms, be open and friendly with them, recognise their power as ambassadors, not just for the school but for the child-centred approach to education, the breadth of the curriculum, all the many advances which have been like sepia photographs bursting into colour. The same head will have a visiting teacher in turn in governors' meetings, demystifying the business of the governing body and allowing teachers to talk about their work. S/he will encourage governors to come in if they can to staff meetings and in-service events, and arrange social meetings for governors and staff. S/he will also encourage teacher governors to act as a bridge between the governing body and the staff and to make a genuine effort to represent colleagues.

Building your own bridges
Few of us are so lucky, though we may get the odd bit of luck now and then. At the other extreme there are dangerous misapprehensions in the staff room about what governors are up to, a certain amount of paranoia about governors' presence in the school, a determination to keep as far away as possible, or - a not uncommon variant - a head who seems to feel threatened by governors getting too

chummy with teachers. This may be a school where there is a very hierarchical structure of school decision-making and not much involvement of junior teachers. Occasionally, in the latter case, governors will be plagued by various forms of tale-telling and grumbling, which should - hard as it sometimes seems - be discouraged. Governors can do more harm than good by carrying half-understood complaints whose source is all too obvious, and it doesn't in the end help teachers, who ought to be brave enough to fight for involvement and at least use their own representatives properly in approaching governors.

If relationships with teachers are not close, or even discouraged, it may be that you face a long and patient process of bridge-building. This chapter gives you an ideal to aim at. In different schools the approach will vary.

Teacher governors

Teacher governors are of course the ready-made bridge if they are brave enough and feel secure enough to tackle serious problems. In one school I know teacher governors not only bring staff concerns fearlessly to governors but also fix up contact opportunities for governors to come into school and spend time with teachers. At the start this should only be done with staff who are compatible and likely to enjoy the experience, because in any enterprise you can only build on confidence: it's no good trying to force contact on the terrified. 'Come and listen to Alison's lesson on pupils' relationships with their parents' to a governor really interested in personal and social education, on behalf of a confident and skilled teacher, is an invitation which makes a friend for life. This is the beginning of more structured contact, since other staff will be encouraged and governors enthused. Observation of classes is the most valuable contact, once fear has been overcome. Chapter 11 suggests some forms of regular governor involvement based on such observation, and every governing body should try to move towards a system of this kind, with sensitivity and care.

Teacher governors can also help by reporting back to colleagues on governors' discussions in a helpful way and conveying governors' desire to have staff opinions on relevant matters, and work steadily towards more organised contact.

Teachers and the governing body

It is good practice to have teachers present in turn at governors' meetings to talk about their area of work - good education for governors, good practice for teachers, and an exercise in mutual understanding. A curriculum working party of governors should work within a frame of a regular review of all the school's work and activity in turn, with teachers invited to talk about their work, their plans, their needs. Teachers should be invited to serve as co-opted members of governors' committees and working parties in suitable cases, as well as teacher governors being routinely members of such groups. Governors should encourage the school to invite them to staff meetings where relevant issues are being discussed, and to in-service events. Governors should always be watchful about issues they are discussing which may cause alarm or misunderstanding among staff, and make sure proper communication is organised.

Social events

Teachers' time is often under pressure these days, but well-chosen opportunities for social contact should not be missed. One governing body had a regular tea-time with staff - just half an hour after school - and took it in turn to bring a cake or some scones. Another provided a breakfast party now and then out of its training budget to talk about school issues in an informal atmosphere and without the pressure of an agenda. Sometimes refreshments half an hour before governors' meetings (depending on the time they take place and the kind of area) make a good opportunity to mix with staff. Governors should choose a time and occasion which is appropriate to the circumstances of the school and not likely to add to teachers' burdens. Nor is it appropriate to see social events as an end in themselves - if they are no more they can be awkward, ambiguous, pointless. They are friendly and constructive only in a context of continuing discussion about the things teachers and governors exist to promote, and trusting communication across the boundaries of our work.

When conflict is unavoidable

Governors are moving inexorably into the standards agenda, with their clear responsibility for school improvement, target-setting, and soon the gradual implementation of performance management, not to mention the injunction to reduce exclusion rates. It would be wrong to suggest that happy relationships will in these areas always come naturally, or can be improved by a kind word or a home-made cake. It will be hard work, because governors must see that they get the strategic information they need to judge the school's standards, must be frank about its needs, and occasionally will have to confront competence issues. The vital thing is to be as transparent as possible in all their thinking and decision-making, so that teachers know exactly how that thinking progresses and the reasons for decisions. The maximum debate must be sought as well as all the human touches. When a really unpopular decision has to be made, perhaps a hard choice to meet budget constraints or an inability to accept a permanent exclusion and thereby challenging a teacher's judgement, it's all-important to show how the decision was reached, what the options were, as well as how governors hated it all. I think it's a good habit for the chair or other representative to speak to all the staff in such cases and at least put a human face on a difficult choice.

All governors will hope that these dramas don't happen often, and that they will have been eased by the ordinary daily friendliness fore and aft.

Thoughtfulness about teachers

Don't forget just ordinary human kindness and courtesy. Remember to congratulate a teacher who has acquired an additional qualification or been responsible for a curriculum development. Thank those who have helped organise a social or fund-raising activity with parents or pupils. Take an interest in teachers' working environment and try to improve it. Show concern for their career development and in-service training. Make sure all your policies on pay and promotion are open and consistent. There is nothing worse than the suspicion that important decisions about one's career are made in secret or on a whim. By their openness and interest governing bodies will win the most important thing of all – the staff's trust.

RELATIONSHIPS WITH THE LEA

Until the late 1980s Local Education Authorities had enormous power in schools. Apart from a small allowance to each school for paper, books, chalk, etc. they handled the budget, decided on the staffing structure and pupil-teacher ratios, looked after the building, and acted as personnel officer for the staff. Between them and school governing bodies there could be tensions, but there was also someone to blame when governors couldn't provide their pupils and teachers with everything they needed.

The relationship between the LEA and today's governing bodies, in schools which are largely self-managing, is bound to be different. Yet the LEA still has an important role. The School Standards and Framework Act 1998 spelled out very clearly not only its task of organising the total school provision for the area to meet its varied needs, but also its responsibility for raising standards of achievement, and indeed producing for government approval concrete plans for doing so. At the same time there has been an extension of OFSTED inspections to cover whole LEA areas, and provision to take power away from those causing concern.

Meanwhile the individual school enjoys (if that is the word!) almost total delegation of funds and the associated accountability. The LEA can still supply a range of services, but schools decide whether or not to buy them. Yet most schools rely on their LEA for a great deal of guidance on legal, financial and personnel matters. The relationship between 'them and us' has always been close and the magnitude of the changes has been slow to sink in.

Even now there is great variety in the relationships from one area to another, depending on the political character of the LEA, on how large and/or scattered its population, its individual style and history and how it reacts to the recent changes. On the last point, some have clung more fiercely to their influence on schools, even at extremes assuming functions they don't really have any more! Others have gone even further than the law requires in distancing themselves from the detail of running schools. All have in different ways found it hard to see what their role will be in the long run and are suffering some sense of insecurity. This chapter is therefore difficult to write in that the experience of governors will vary and in that one must search for the permanent and positive features of this still vital relationship.

A new start for 'them and us'

One of the features of the relationship which must change is one which most school governors grew up with: namely, the sense of largely helpless governing bodies, trapped in a web of bureaucracy, victims of a skinflint paymaster and having the appearance of power without the reality. I am talking about the 'them and us' mentality. That now has little meaning, partly because the LEA itself has only limited freedom of action and partly because most of the total schools budget is passed down to governors to do their best with. The total amount available for local spending is largely controlled by central government and is also greatly complicated by the amount of extra money that schools can 'bid' for within particular centrally administered programmes. Another new feature is the growing influence of private finance in individual schools and even whole areas.

If governors managing budgets suffer frustration in what they see as a hopeless task, the LEA may not be able to help it, and their MP may be better able to act on their complaints. As for bureaucracy, there is very little in governing bodies' work which is not within their control if they want it to be. The one exception perhaps is on the capital works side where priorities and projects are still the LEA's affair, though even these need government sanction if they are large projects and come out of a government allocation if they are small ones. Otherwise the debate, if there is a debate, has shifted to the share of the cake which education gets locally compared with other services, and the fine detail of the budget formula. Increasingly governors are setting up organisations of their own within the LEA to maintain a friendly and constructive dialogue with the LEA about common problems and concerns. This could be a new kind of relationship, with governors and LEAs working together to improve the local service.

The family grows up

At this moment in history LEAs are like parents of a family growing up. Their schools have to stand on their own feet more so than in the past. A wise parent will have set a good example, talked about the principles by which they hope the young people will live their lives, offered information and guidance but not too forcefully. If this has all been well done the 'children' will come and visit, will ask for help when they need it, and will remember the guidance they have been given.

Support in managing the school

It is still to the LEA that their schools must look for support and guidance in managing the budget and to them that they should initially make representations about things they feel are not fair. The LEA also provides much of the information on which school budget decisions are based, and now that some of the teething troubles of Local Management of Schools are behind us, there is scope for governors to make their needs known and to say if the form in which they get information could be more helpful in keeping track of the money.

Expertise

The expertise which governors need from the LEA goes far beyond the financial management of the school, however. LEAs have almost a century of experience in managing not just money, but property, personnel and children's learning, all of which governors badly need. The LEA which is attuned to the future will be considering how best to present and market this essential information to schools. All too often simple language is not a feature of official documents, and in this too governors should make their needs known and try to encourage a move to simpler and more homely communication.

There is always expert advice available to governors who ask for it, though in many areas of work they can no longer be forced to take it. In the work of staff selection and personnel management, in particular, most governors will feel that they need help. The Chief Education Officer has the right to be present or represented, and to advise, when senior staff are being chosen, and in this vital task such advice is needed by most governors.

LEAs will have guidelines on staff discipline procedures, redundancy, and many other issues which are associated with the governors' new role. It is important to remember that if, say, in dismissing a member of staff, the governors are supported by the LEA in their decision, any costs which might arise as a result of a successful appeal to an industrial tribunal may be borne by the LEA. If, however, the governors act contrary to LEA advice and the case goes wrong on them, any costs will fall on the school budget.

At some time most governors will come up against problems concerning the performance of the school which are hard to tackle without help. The work in one year or subject may seem to be falling below the general standard of the school. The reason will rarely be simple, and a trained eye may be needed to help governors take the necessary action. The LEA is there to help with expert advice but is no longer the sole provider: governors can buy in the expertise they want from other LEAs or private agencies, a competitive situation which some LEAs have adapted to more quickly than others.

Working to the rules

Until a few years ago most community and controlled school governing bodies were clerked by officers of the LEA. The presence of a clerk of this sort of standing was welcome to most governing bodies, while others found it intrusive.

Now, however, the government requires LEAs to give governors a small sum of money to buy this service. In some areas the LEA still offers the service and governors can buy it if they wish. In others the LEA has given up clerking, and governing bodies make their own arrangements. One loss resulting from the decline of the LEA clerking service is that there is often nobody at a meeting who can guide governors, and they are very much on their own, sometimes unsure of their powers or the proper procedures. Uncertainty can lead to abuse of power by strong members of the group.

I think it is important that LEAs should take this responsibility of being the friendly bobby on the beat very seriously, and replace in some way the service which came automatically with the clerk. Sometimes an inspector is attached to a school and attends governors' meetings. If briefed to do so, such a person could help develop governors' shared understanding of the rules.

Maintaining good relationships

The third vital role a good LEA can play is that of a guardian of good relationships. If the LEA accepts that the quality of learning in a school and its efficient management are no longer under its direct control, it will also accept that relationships are a major factor with the school. Partnership has replaced direction, so if the LEA is responsible for effectiveness it will make partnership a key objective. This is very simple and obvious, but rarely acted upon. Officers and inspectors will talk among themselves about schools where relationships are poor, but rarely tackle them head-on. The LEA has the power to advise and to warn, to chide and to set ground-rules for sharing. At extremes a governing body can be made totally ineffective by the uncooperative behaviour of an individual - a misguided or inconsiderate governor, an over-dominant chair, or a head who hasn't begun to share responsibility with governors. Governors sometimes need help from outside with these situations, not pussy-footing.

Accountability

Governors must of course keep the LEA informed about their decisions and their problems. They must also account for their use of the school budget. You will know that governors are not allowed to plan to run on a deficit, but if it happens, any deficit (or surplus) which occurs is carried forward. Provided governors have acted in good faith they need not be afraid of their responsibility. In the unlikely event of a governing body having been totally irresponsible and negligent - and one hopes that action would have been taken before things went so far - the LEA has power to take their financial powers away from them.

What governors can do

Much of what has been said concerns the LEA's changing role and how, ideally, they should work with their governors, just as parts of the book point to how head teachers and other partners in school government should relate to the governing ideal. Firstly, it is helpful in what is sometimes a bewildering set of relationships to have a picture of the ideal. That gives you confidence in moving forward, knowing you are not being unreasonable. It also guides your questions and requests, your responses and your occasional complaints. A governing body with a clear view of what it wants (and doesn't want) from the LEA is halfway to achieving it, especially in a situation where some LEAs are themselves working out a new role. To sum up:

- **Governors of LEA schools are responsible to the LEA for their effective management of the school's resources and its standards.**

- **In this task they have a great deal of independence, and provided they carry out their legal responsibilities and respond to any requests from information concerning those responsibilities which central or local government require, they are free to organise their meetings, their agenda and their general management of their business as they wish - they are responsible for their own rule-keeping.**

- **Nevertheless, it would be an unusual governing body which did not sometimes need carefully targeted expert advice - on money, premises, law and insurance, personnel management and school performance. The very best may be available in the home LEA. But governors must remember that they are the customers now, they can buy elsewhere if they wish, and the LEA must remember this too. A new tradition must be frank exchanges about quality - if the guidance isn't good or the language inaccessible governors must say so. Even in a free market the local shop could become the best - if it knows what customers want. Local shopping is easier, and so is the home LEA if good enough.**

- **It is vital that the LEA helps governing bodies with their rule-keeping and with their relationships both within the governing body and with the head and professional staff.**

- **Above all governing bodies must make full use of the training available. The best governor training in LEAs is first class, and includes in-house team-building sessions and help-lines as well as off-site courses. Let your local governor support team know your needs and take full advantage of what is offered. Complain if it isn't good enough.**

PART THREE: RULES

 9   ## HOW DO GOVERNING BODIES WORK?

....Together

There is one over-ridingly important answer to the question above - TOGETHER. It is an answer which has several meanings and they run through this book like coal seams, hard and shiny.

Most obviously, governors are a team, not a collection of individuals or groups with separate agendas. However much they may differ in the opinions and experience they start with, they are united by commitment to the school and the responsibility they share for its well-being. In short, they have a common purpose.

In another and strictly legal sense governing bodies also work together. Individual governors have no power to do anything except in fulfilment of the governing body's will. The work of the governing body takes the form of decisions which governors make together at a meeting, by consensus or if necessary by majority vote, and the law lays down all sorts of rules:

- how many have to be present before the decision is legal (called a quorum)
- which decisions may be entrusted to a small group and which must be taken by all the governors.
- when a governor has to keep out of a discussion because of a special interest in the outcome.

There are also rules about the length of notice of meetings, chair and vice-chair, and other details. These we shall come to later.

Here the point to emphasise is that whenever governors get into a mess it is nearly always because individual members, often with good if confused motives, have tried to do things off their own bat, because the governing body has been vague or casual about letting its responsibility slip away - or more particularly - because powerful individuals or groups have manipulated the rest into letting go of their share of responsibility. Only the governing body has power of decision and of action.

The third sense in which governors work together is in loyalty to one another and the decisions they make democratically as a body.

You may as an individual totally disagree with the decision the majority have taken, but you failed to convince them so you lost. That is that, at least unless and until the matter comes up again. You must do nothing to interfere with action taken on that decision or discredit it. You must not by word or deed try to undermine the unity of your governing body in public.

.... Openly

The law intends that nearly all governors' work is conducted openly and that any member of the public is able to see the papers leading up to the decision. If the governing body wishes to make an item confidential, because it interferes with the privacy of individuals (e.g. by revealing details about their health, financial affairs, private lives) or for some other quite exceptional reason, it must make a clear decision to that effect, and on these items all governors' lips must be sealed. On unclassified items (and anything not expressly classified is open) there is no reason why decisions should not be reported after the meeting, provided the report is scrupulously accurate and does not reveal any of the detail about how individuals lined up or about personal indiscretions of any kind.

> **Remember, confidentiality is intended to be exceptional and mainly for the protection of individual privacy. It is not a good enough reason that an item is controversial or disclosure inconvenient.**

As for visitors to meetings, the governing body is at liberty to open its meeting to any visitors or to invite such visitors as it chooses. Only the governing body makes this decision, as with decisions about confidentiality - not the LEA, not the chair, not the head teacher. Both are shared decisions.

...On a basis of equality

All governors have equal status. It should not be necessary to say this, but there are many examples of governors feeling like second-class governors for different reasons and of attempts to restrict the role of for example parent governors (because they might gossip, because the decision affects children in their child's year, because they don't have professional knowledge or skill) or teacher governors (because the finance committee decisions affect teachers' departmental budgets or because the post to be filled is senior to theirs).

> **The law intends that all governors should make an equal contribution and be equally valued and equally trusted.**

There are restrictions in the law on what an individual governor can participate in but either these apply to everyone (like the rules on withdrawing because of special interest - more details on page 47 and 48) or they are very exceptional. For instance, no employee of the school may be chair or vice-chair. That is because s/he might have a special professional interest in so many items of business that it would be difficult for her/him to do the job. Co-opted governors in LEA schools may not vote when other co-options are being considered. This is to ensure that a group which in many schools could be a large group and whose members are not elected, does not risk becoming a clique. Finally, the chair has certain very limited extra powers, such as being able to make decisions in a real emergency when the school is for any reason at risk. Otherwise the chair, like any other governor, can only make a decision or take an action if the governing body has specifically asked him or her to do so, and if it is something it can legally delegate.

...In short, democratically

That word hasn't been used before because it is really what all the others add up to.

Acting together and only together, being loyal to majority decisions, working as openly as possible, ensuring that every member is treated and trusted equally and encouraged to contribute equally to what will become shared policies, are all elements in working democratically.

In the section which follows more detail is given about the rules which underpin the teamwork of governing bodies. They are not rules for the sake of rules. If you look at them carefully you will see that they all have something to do with the important principles set out in this section. The rules in chapter 10 all work to keep responsibility firmly in the hands of a governing body working in unity, to prevent power from slipping into too few hands, to protect the right of individuals to contribute equally with the minimum restrictions, and to ensure that decisions are made thoughtfully, fairly and openly.

ARE YOU A GOOD TEAM?

Ask yourselves these questions about your team

- Do you know about the skills and experience of your colleagues?

- Do they know about yours?

- Can you have a healthy disagreement and keep your shared aims?

- Do you talk often about what you value in the school and your aims for it? Do you spend enough time establishing principles and good practices, rather than meeting every issue head-on?

- Do you feel that every governor contributes?

- Are you satisfied that there are no governors with private agendas?

- Do all governors leave the meeting feeling they have had a say?

- Do you have good systems of work-sharing involving everybody?

- Are all interest groups fairly represented on committees?

- Do your teacher governors contribute confidently and without fear?

- Would someone always intervene to protect a governor who was for any reason being prevented from making a full contribution?

- Do you have a system for every governor to commit some regular time to involvement in the school? Or do you feel there are some who won't?

- Do you spend enough time organising your work properly?

- Do you feel that you have a free choice of chair?

- Does your chair see his/her main role as team-building?

- Are you always clear about what you have decided?

- Do you spend enough time looking forward or are you agenda-driven?

- Do you realise that looking ahead is the only way to make sure you are involved at the proper item, and not too late?

- Are you all loyal to majority decisions?

10   **IMPORTANT RULES**

These rules are the most important among the new regulations made under the 1998 School Standards and Framework Act (Statutory Instrument 2163 of 1999). The regulations have the force of law.

1. Meetings Governors must meet at least once a term: most will need to meet more often. Seven days' notice is required, with the Agenda and relevant papers. At the first meeting of the school year the governing body must elect a Chair and Vice-Chair. Neither of these can be a person employed at the school. Governors must also at least once a year review their committee arrangements - elect members and agree terms of reference and methods of working. The Chair may call a special meeting without the usual period of notice if necessary, and if any three governors request a special meeting, the clerk must arrange it as soon as possible.

2. Your clerk The clerk has to be chosen by the governing body. This office cannot now be held by a serving governor. A clerk can be dismissed by a decision of the whole governing body.

3. Making decisions The governing body's responsibilities are corporate: the only legal decisions are those made together at properly convened meetings or delegated within the regulations. Governors as individuals have no power, except, in an emergency, the Chair. (See *Powers of the Chair* below) Decisions are made after discussion by general agreement or majority vote. The Chair has a second or casting vote if votes for and against are equal. In some circumstances a governor may not be able to play a part in making a decision because of conflict of interest. (See *Conflict of Interest* below.)

4. The head teacher is a full member of the governing body unless s/he decides otherwise. The head may attend all meetings of the governing body and its committees, except when they relate to the appointment of his/her successor or where there is a conflict of interest, e.g. when a decision is being made on an excluded pupil. This applies whether or not the head chooses to be a governor.

5. Role of the Chair The Chair provides leadership for the governing body but has no powers to act on their behalf without instructions except in an emergency, and even then only if the action is one which may legally be delegated (See *Delegation* below). An emergency is defined as a situation which threatens the well-being of the school or any pupil, parent or staff member and where there is no time to call a special meeting. The governing body has power to remove the Chair from office if there is widespread dissatisfaction among them: the detailed procedures are rigorous (e.g. they spread over two meetings, there is full provision for reasons to be given and replied to and the higher level of quorum applies.) If the Chair resigns or is removed mid-term, there must be an election: the Vice-Chair does not automatically inherit.

6. Quorum To make a legal decision a certain proportion of governors must be present. For most matters this is one third of the total membership (including vacancies) but for certain decisions a higher quorum of two thirds of governors in post and eligible to vote is required. The main decisions requiring a higher quorum relate to co-opting or otherwise appointing a governor, and delegating functions.

7. Non-attendance A governor who, without the permission of the governing body, has not attended a meeting for six months, is automatically disqualified. If it is an LEA or representative governor, a foundation governor or a co-opted governor, s/he may not be reappointed to the same governing body in that capacity for 12 months. In order to make disqualification mean something, governors must always record, when a member apologises for absence, that they accept the apology and the reasons. Otherwise it does not count.

8. Delegation Governors are allowed to delegate some functions to individuals or committees, but there are many exceptions which are given in full in your Guide to the Law. Among those which cannot be delegated are:

a) alteration, closure or change of character of school;

b) appointment of chair and vice-chair;

c) forming committees and delegating functions;

d) submitting the budget to the LEA each year;

e) co-opting, appointing, or removing governors;

f) ratifying choice of new head or deputy;

g) arranging appeals against dismissal;

h) policies on admission, school discipline, collective worship, sex education, charging for activities, fixing school terms, holidays and times of sessions;

i) delegating functions to an Education Action Forum or requesting their reinstatement;

j) agreeing the annual report to parents, the prospectus and the home-school agreement.

9. Committees Governors are required to set up a committee of at least three members (but see note) for staff discipline and one of five members for pupil exclusions, and such other committees as they think fit. For staff discipline they also need a second committee to consider any appeal, and this must exclude governors on the first committee or any others with prior knowledge. Any appeal committee must have no fewer members than the committee which made the decision. (NOTE. Exceptionally, in very small schools where there are less than six governors eligible, the governing body may itself decide on the size of discipline committees, subject to the second committee always having no fewer members than the first. In practice this means that a first committee of two is acceptable and an appeal committee of two or three).

Non-governors may be co-opted to committees with the governing body's agreement in each individual case, but governors are always in a majority and only governors may chair a committee. No employee of the school may chair a committee with delegated power.

Every committee must have a clerk, but, except in the statutory committees, it may be a member of the governing body. Committees must always record their decisions and report to the full governing body.

Governors employed at the school may be involved in discussion of *policies* on pay and staff appraisal, but not in any discussion of the pay or appraisal of an individual.

10. Rescinding a Resolution If at any meeting a governing body rescinds a resolution made at a previous meeting, the item must have been on the published agenda for the second meeting as a specific item.

11. Co-options Co-opted governors may not vote in future co-options. Since September 1999 staff of the school have not been eligible to be co-opted governors.

12. Removal of governors There are new provisions allowing some types of governor to be removed if this is the wish of a majority of colleagues. Elected (i.e. parent and teacher governors) cannot be removed at all, and LEA and foundation governors can only be removed (for sufficient reason) by the body they represent. Co-opted governors can, however, be removed by resolution of the governing body to which they were co-opted or, in the case of additional co-opted sponsorship governors, on the recommendation of the appointing body (in this case the removal must, however, also have the support of the governing body). The procedure has to be spread over two meetings, with fourteen days at least between. In each case the removal must be clearly included on the agenda as an item of business and a resolution must be passed. The governor or governors proposing the removal must give reasons, and the governor concerned must be given an opportunity to respond. If then a resolution to remove is confirmed, the person ceases to be a governor. Exactly the same procedure applies to the removal from office (but not in this case from the governing body) of the Chair, if there is widespread dissatisfaction among colleagues with his/her performance.

13. Conflict of interest A governor may play no part in a discussion, or vote, if he or she has a pecuniary interest in the outcome, a conflict of interest, or there are circumstances which raise reasonable doubt about his/her ability to be impartial. Anyone who is in a position to give evidence on a matter under discussion e.g. a witness to a disciplinary incident, may, however, be heard by the relevant committee, but if the circumstances are such that that person could not be impartial (e.g. in the case of a pupil, the parents of a victim) s/he takes no part in the decision. By the same token, although the head teacher would probably present the school's case beforehand in an exclusion case, s/he would withdraw while the decision is made.

14 .Visitors to meetings, governors' papers, and confidentiality Observers may attend governors' meetings if the governing body so decides. Governors' agenda and papers, and minutes once the Chair has approved them, must be available for any interested party to see, with any confidential items excluded. Only the governing body may decide to classify an item as confidential. Classification is intended primarily to protect the privacy of individuals, and it is clearly intended that it should not be used excessively. Governors may disclose non-confidential decisions - but it is vital that they do so accurately and discreetly. It is not good practice to reveal the detail of what individuals said or how they voted, or in any way to be disloyal to colleagues or put the governing body in a bad light.

15. General **These rules are not dry examples of bureaucratic thinking. If you look at them carefully you will see that they are all designed to protect the corporate nature of governors' powers and the integrity of their decisions. They prevent power drift, the process by which individuals or groups assume too much power. They ensure that in general governors have an equal right to contribute (particularly teacher and other staff governors), but that exceptionally when an individual might have an axe to grind that person plays no part. They make certain that when a governing body gives power to some person or group - whether it's co-opting a colleague or delegating a task to a group - or takes certain particularly important decisions, it does so consciously and carefully, with enough members present. The rules are in short safeguards for the democratic working of the governing body. If all are not equally familiar with them, or they are not taken seriously, it opens the door to abuse of power at best and at worst illegal decisions which could be challenged in a damaging way by aggrieved individuals, by the courts, by local authorities or the Secretary of State.**

WAS IT A GOOD MEETING?

Try this short series of questions after your meetings

- Were any new members or visitors welcomed and clearly introduced?

- Did you have all the important papers in advance of the meeting?

- Did your chair seem to have a clear plan for the meeting?

- Did s/he seek governors' agreement to any changes in the order of items and about the time to be allocated to items?

- Were you satisfied that the agenda represented the vital matters which needed to be discussed? Would you know how to get an item on the agenda?

- Were you clear about the issues involved in the items discussed?

- Did your chair set out clearly what the options were?

- Were irrelevant or rambling contributions pleasantly curtailed?

- Do you think all governors left the meeting satisfied with the outcome and without feeling they had been prevented from contributing?

- Was there any effort to share work and responsibility even-handedly?

- Was the head brought into the discussion when appropriate?

- Were you satisfied that you were not being manipulated, given half a story, or asked to approve something that had already been sewn up?

- Did your chair make sure everyone was happy before assuming agreement?

- At the end were you clear about what had been decided, who was to take action, by when, and how you would be informed that it had been done?

- On any item where the wording was crucial, did you guide your clerk?

- Were you looking forward to items you would need to discuss, so that you could organise yourselves, ensure that proper information was provided, and that consultation was carried out in time?

- Did you feel that the meeting had moved things on in a helpful way?

- **Was it going to improve the learning of children in the school?**

11   GETTING TO KNOW YOUR SCHOOL

There is no substitute for direct observation of children learning, and I will stick my neck out and say that any governor who can't manage it at all, ever, should think again about whether s/he is suitable. I know we still have a long way to go with the problem of time. We need to convince government that if it is serious about participation by all types of people we must have a legal right to paid time to get involved.

Meanwhile we must spread the message among employers that governors are important, and publicise the growing number of firms who are generous with time for their governor-employees. Until we win this battle it will be very difficult for a hard core of mainly hourly paid people, with unsympathetic employers and three weeks' holiday with limited choice of when it's taken, and also for the poorer self-employed, to play their part without hardship. Outside the hard core there are the professionals with six weeks' annual leave, those on flexi-time or shift work, the unemployed, the better-off self-employed, those in the enlightened companies mentioned, and some in small firms which are informal enough for friends to cover for one another. All need to accept that being a governor means willingness to spare such time as you can to visit the school.

Big events are not enough

Nearly all governors try to go to the big events - the school play, the Christmas concert, the leavers' party, the community's festivals. This is important for pride and belonging, for that lump in the throat without whose occasional presence we probably couldn't face the frustrations. But important as they are, the big events don't help you make better decisions.

Neither is 'dropping in any time'

Many well-meaning heads assure their governors that they are always glad to see them and urge them to drop in any time. They are often disappointed. But the same invitation from a casual acquaintance you met in the street wouldn't produce results either if you didn't know what time they got in from work, whether they had a sleep before they did anything, what television programmes they watched, what time they had their meal, what hour they went to bed, which evening mother came round. It is very hard for an outsider to drop in on a complicated organisation like a school without feeling awkward, and a visit without a plan or a focus isn't likely to be much of a learning experience anyway.

Every governing body needs a system

Quite apart from the lack of learning experience in a casual visit, individual governors have no automatic right of entry to schools. Some, not perhaps as welcome as those mentioned above, have found themselves in trouble by assuming that a governor is some kind of inspector and entitled to take schools by surprise. We have already noted that individually governors have no power, and come into schools to **learn**, not to *judge*. They need to visit, but they do so either when invited by the head or in accordance with some plan agreed by the whole governing body. They will of course be courteous and careful not to disrupt the school's normal activity.

Practical advice on visiting

Since visits need to have a focus, it isn't enough for governing bodies to establish a simple system of visiting governor under which it guarantees only that a member will visit the school at predetermined intervals. The individual visit must have a focus. Apart from this, it doesn't matter what system is adopted as long as it satisfies the following criteria:

- it must provide some observation of the learning process
- it must encourage the governor who wants to be involved
- it must be a prop for the governor who means well but tends to put things off
- it must in time discourage the governor who doesn't really want this kind of involvement
- it must break up undesirable concentrations of power on the governing body by giving each governor some responsibility.

The point about discouraging governors with no real commitment may seem harsh, but if a governing body develops an *involvement culture* it is essential that it drops passengers. This is a peaceful process if any system the governors adopt is linked to reports by visiting governors at full meetings. In other words, there must be an element of peer group pressure, otherwise known as public shame. *In slimming clubs it isn't the diet sheet which does the trick, but the public weighing.* No system runs itself.

Some schools give every governor a special area of interest - sport, the arts, special needs. That provides a set of events to take an interest in and a focus for visits. Primary schools often find it helpful to link a governor to a class, especially good if the governor goes up with the class, seeing the whole curriculum develop and getting to know a group of children really well, not only hearing reading and going on visits but exchanging birthday cards and going to see the new baby. Others have adopted a 'duty governor of the month' system, whereby each governor, well in advance and with the chance to negotiate or swap, accepts that for one month of the school year the school will call on him or her (not the chair) to attend the small event, plant the tree, give out the cycling proficiency badges, take part in the selection panel for a teacher.

This is particularly good in meeting the criterion about spreading the power, since it distributes chairing duties around. The duty governor also promises to spend a little time in the school during working hours, looking at one subject or activity which lends itself to a planned visit. One school combined this with shadowing a teacher - but this was when confidence had grown and at the staff's request. Even then it only involved volunteers.

Obviously visits need some preparation, with visitor and staff understanding the purpose - especially that governors come in to learn - and the visitor knowing which activity or lesson is to be the focus, whom they will meet and where, and a little about how the lesson or activity fits into the syllabus.

Apart from its value as a learning process, this idea helps to de-mystify governors in teachers' eyes and build relationships. It is an expression of the high expectations which a wise head will have of governors and governors of one another.

Other ways of learning
Governors can also learn a great deal from the written word, and should encourage the head teacher to include them in the circulation of all routine school communications. Regular newsletters to parents, calendars of school events, lists of sporting fixtures, communications about outings or residential visits, all help to give a flavour of the school. One very good idea is for every governor to have a named folder in the school office, into which is slipped every communication as it comes out. Governors visit the school when convenient (and preferably regularly!) to empty their folders. This takes almost no extra time for school staff and has the added advantage of bringing governors in. Attendance at staff meetings and in-service events are other excellent ways of getting to know the school.

12   BECOMING A BETTER TEAM

In Chapters 9 and 10 we talked about the principles of unity, openness and equality on which governors should establish themselves, and we have looked at the rules by which they work. Chapter 11 gave some practical suggestions for becoming better informed about the school. This, too, is a very practical chapter about team-building, organisation and work-sharing.

Valuing one another

A governing body is a collection of people with a commitment to the school. In this respect members are equal, whatever the differences of their experience or education, and they will work well if this is accepted by all. Governors with a little more experience should plan properly to welcome new colleagues. Before they even start it is a good idea for a colleague to telephone or visit and offer to collect them for the first meeting, talk over the agenda in advance, lend them any books or materials which he or she has found particularly helpful. If there is a training session soon, offer to accompany them. The head should invite them to come into school and sort out a few key documents for them. The chair should find out a little about their interests.

On the day of the first meeting, why not meet half an hour earlier for a cup of tea and a sandwich, for old and new governors to get to know each other? When the meeting starts, the chair should make sure all governors introduce themselves clearly and fully, saying something about themselves and how they got involved.

New governors, or more experienced governors who remain timid, should be brought into the discussion often. Jargon should be avoided and any unfamiliar words or abbreviations de-coded, without being patronising. Make sure too much cosiness doesn't exclude anybody. If first names are used, or there are 'in' jokes, everybody should be treated in the same way.

Any skills governors bring to the job - and I don't mean just word-processing or accounts but being a good listener or peacemaker or organiser, mending things or speaking another language - should be put to use soon, and new governors should be included on committees or working parties straight away. You may feel you need an experienced chair to start these small groups off, but make a rule that new governors should be considered for such jobs before the year is out.

At meetings all contributions should be given equal attention and respect. Make sure nobody is held back by shyness. Evidence of any special interest should be taken up: when possible give that person a suitable task. Even if people don't speak, make sure they agree with what is proposed before assuming there is no disagreement.

Your respect for each other has its final expression in your loyalty to decisions you have made as a group and your willingness to implement them wholeheartedly even if you yourself had doubts about them. This is the mark of a real team.

Looking ahead

Governors are always tempted to lurch straight into that long agenda. This leads to poor decisions if they have never talked about their principles and priorities, never stepped back to think about what's more important to them, what they are trying to achieve, and how they are going to organise themselves. These will be the governors who haven't any written policies, have not produced the development plan but left it to the head, and because they are never ready with alternative plans are manipulated by anyone with an axe to grind. They will assume that any solution which falls into their lap is the right one.

At the beginning of the year especially, and again at the beginning of each meeting, get the head to talk about the issues coming up for the school before you meet again. Then you can plan your work so that you are not always commenting on things it's too late to change. Before you appoint a chair, talk about the sort of chair you want, what qualities are important, how much you all want to be involved. Talk often about the school, what seem to you to be the special things about it, what you want to protect and promote. If you solve a budget problem without discussion by not filling that drama post or by down-grading that special needs co-ordinator vacancy, your are letting events drive you. You should have talked long ago about how important drama and special needs were to you. Then you might not have panicked.

Sharing the work

When you set up committees or working parties, be sure you are only delegating what you legally can, and make your instructions precise. Make sure all interest groups are fairly spread over all committees. In so many schools there is one powerful committee - finance, usually - and it's all male LEA or business governors. Spread out the parents and teachers over all tasks, and experienced and new governors too.

Never lose an opportunity to get a small group of people looking in more detail at an issue. Make sure these groups communicate well with the governing body so that responsibility doesn't slip away. It's a good idea if all committees are open, with a core membership, but all governors knowing when they are meeting and welcome to attend. This removes any suspicion that power is in too few hands.

When documents come to governors for action, share them out at random so that all governors get to take one home, bring it back smartly if it seems urgent but otherwise find out if it's for information, action or comment and how it fits into what the school does now, and present it at the meeting. That governor might also take follow-up action. Again there is often a suspicion, which this will cure, that not all governors see important documents.

Avoiding A and B teams

All this is about A and B teams, which many governors say they have. Sometimes the A team doesn't even know it looks like this, or alternatively would love to be able to interest more people and lighten its own load. But suspicion is destructive even if unfounded.

Note also what is said in chapter 11 about getting to know the school.

Making space for colleagues

As well as making sure that new or shy colleagues are made to feel at home, it's important to keep an eye open for particular groups or members who might have more long-term problems in making a full contribution, In particular, read what is said about parent and teacher governors in chapter 4 on representing others, and make sure that your are aware of any tendency to restrict the role of your parent and teacher representatives or their right to communicate with their groups. Often a colleague from a different group can gently press their case for involvement or encourage them to speak for those who elected them. An innocent question like *'Do parents seem to be concerned about this?' 'What is the view in the staff room?'* or *'Shouldn't we ask one of the teacher governors to be on the committee on pay?'* is often all you need. If you are yourself a parent or teacher governor, remember that you are in your own way a privileged person because you have direct knowledge of the school, and some LEA and especially some co-opted governors may feel a bit left out, especially if they find it really hard to get to daytime events. Be on the look-out for opportunities to get them involved or give them insights and explanations.

Don't make a mystery of money

There's nothing more divisive than money if you allow it to be too much of a mystery. Everybody manages money at some level from an early age, and the choices schools have to make are not really any different from those we make in our own lives. How much to set aside for the gas bill, new carpets or a holiday? Making sure the children understand that they all get a turn even if it's not right now, and that urgent needs must be met.

There is a natural tendency for 'experts' to make things look difficult, and if experts are making decisions about money seem harder rather than easier, think again about how you use experts, or insist that you do get information in a form you can cope with. Presenting financial decisions in an orderly and helpful way is a job for trained people, but deciding on priorities for spending is not. Every governor can and should contribute to such decisions, and leaving it to people whom you have been told are good at it is a sure recipe for allowing responsibility to slip away. Make sure, too, that within the school there is no muttering about money decisions: staff should be fully aware of the thinking behind all choices and have a chance to put their point of view. *Openness* and *consistency* are vital.

Organising major tasks such as the annual report to parents
If the governing body has a specific piece of work to do, it's obviously sensible to have a small group to keep it moving, chase up contributions and pull it all together for final acceptance. Since nine or nineteen people can't write a report, the only other alternative is to leave it all to some poor individual, most often the head, and that is undesirable. But such a job needs careful planning to make sure that the general shape of the finished product is talked about first and guidance is given to those who put the words together.

Because it's so important and so often inadequate, we'll take as an example the governors' annual report to parents (all too frequently written by the head, which misses the whole point of a distinctive governors' perspective on the school and isn't what the law intended). But even when governors have clearly made an effort, so many reports I have read are monotonous, complacent and uninspiring. The ones that stand out are those where the general plan has been thought about, where many hands have clearly contributed even within a skilled editorial frame, and where the content reflects the school as seen by many eyes.

The occasional report which breathes life and vigour concentrates on the things that matter to parents which aren't often publicised. It doesn't skate over problems in a mistaken fear of slipping down the popularity league (people respond to being included) but honestly seeks understanding or help. It is written in homely and simple language. It may give profiles of the governors and have contributions by individual governors and staff. It will include children's writing and pictures. It will give some sense of how the governors organise their work and what matters to them most in the school. Producing a report like this is the greatest test of a good team, and time spent thinking about the format of the meeting itself and finding strategies which will work in your community is also well worth the effort.

Getting the role of the chair right
If governors' teamwork is poor, it's often because they have accepted too dominant a role for the chair.

The chair's role is vitally important. A good chair is the keeper of the school's vision, the head's friend and confidant, the one responsible for moving the work forward, the inspiration to others, the person who ensures that the meeting is orderly, fair and purposeful, and that time is given to the most important things. But it isn't good if the chair imposes the vision, has a relationship with the head which excludes others, makes all the decisions and discourages debate at a meeting. It is important to remember that the chair has no power to act on behalf of the governors unless (a) they have specifically delegated a task which it is legal to delegate or (b) in a dire emergency like the school being burnt down.

A chair can do purely formal things like planting a tree or thanking the retiring dinner lady or opening the new block. But the chair can't authorise a big purchase or agree to variations in the design of the new building or the suspension of a teacher unless the governors have said so. The chair cannot in any circumstances (even with the governors' permission) agree to a subject being dropped from the curriculum or a pupil being permanently excluded, because curriculum decisions can't legally be made except by all the governors, and permanent exclusion has to be confirmed by a special committee elected by the governors.

We've defined a good chair. An even better chair is all these things but also someone who builds a team, gets the best from others, spreads enthusiasm, shares the work, makes space for every governor to contribute. Remember that you'll have a wider choice of chair if you aren't looking for someone to do all the work for you.

Accepting that if things go wrong it's because you let it happen

This is about taking responsibility for your own rules and your own teamwork. More and more, there isn't any 'somebody' to tell you what to do or to blame if things go wrong. It isn't 'somebody' who put all that junk on the agendas. It isn't 'somebody' who decided that the chair and vice-chair and another powerful governor should select the new head, or elected somebody you didn't want to be chair again. Nor did 'somebody' say in the minutes that governors were a 'little concerned' when really they were hopping mad. It was you. Your meeting, your agendas, your chair, your clerk. Your decision, even if it only happened because you looked at the ceiling, took too long to find your glasses, weren't well enough informed, or too polite. If bad things happen it's because we are slow, too uninformed or too nice.

A sure cure for being too nice is to shut your eyes for a moment and think hard about the children. Think about that small hand clutching the recorder. Think about the tongue out in the corner of the mouth in intense concentration doing the first ever bit of joined-up writing. The festivals of light, the nativity plays, the seven-year-old black Joseph guarding a very pink baby doll in a crib. Or Professor Higgins, fourteen, in 'My Fair Lady', too-large sports jacket, squeaky voice, very unconvincing until he sings 'I've grown accustomed to her face' so sweetly that your throat hurts and suddenly you know that that boy became a man learning about human pain and rejection.

Suddenly it doesn't seem so important that you may offend that old man who's been chair for twenty years, who misses the point and loses his place and asks women applying for teaching jobs if they have to go shopping at lunch-time or what they do when their children are ill. It doesn't seem to matter that a powerful councillor will be devastated if you say quietly, 'Please could we all decide that?' and the clerk put out if you say 'Please, we said "hopping mad"'. Because you will have asked yourself the question 'Which is worse, offending adults or damaging children?', and if the point is an important one the answer is easy.

Indeed, a moment or two thinking about the children makes everything easier, not just accepting responsibility for good teamwork, but putting up with the frustration, missing your favourite TV programme or your supper, getting misunderstood, or just simply keeping at it.

The School Standards and Framework Act 1998

Constitution of governing bodies

From September 1999 every school will have a separate governing body - no more grouping of primary schools as allowed under the 1980 Act and subsequently. The following sets out the details of composition:

GENERAL

In all schools the head teacher shall be governor unless at any time s/he decides otherwise (previously GM heads had no choice of opting out of being a governor). In all primary schools where there is a minor authority one co-opted place must go to a representative of that authority. If there are more than one the governors decide which. Regulations may allow additional co-options in prescribed circumstances.

PRIMARY AND SPECIAL SCHOOLS

A   *Community Primary School* 4 or 5 parent governors, 3 or 4 LEA governors, 1 or 2 teacher governors, 1 support staff governor, 3 or 4 co-opted governors.

B   *Community Primary School under 100 pupils* This is an option - governors to choose between A and B. 3 parent governors, 2 LEA governors, 1 teacher governor, 1 or 0 staff governor, 2 co-opted governors.

C   *Community Special School* May choose between A and B regardless of size. 1 co-opted governor shall be replaced in a hospital school by a representative of the Health Authority or Trust and in any other school by a representative of the Health Authority or Trust and in any other school by a representative of appropriate voluntary organisation(s)

D   *Foundation Primary School* 5 or 6 parent governors, 2 LEA governors, 1 teacher governor, 1 staff governor, 3 or 4 foundation governors, 1 co-opted governor.

E   *Foundation Primary School under 100 pupils* May choose between D and E. 4 parent governors, 2 LEA governors, 1 teacher governor, 1 or 0 staff governor, 2 foundation governors, 1 co-opted governor.

F   *Voluntary Controlled Primary School* 4 or 5 parent governors, 3 LEA governors, 1 teacher governor, 1 staff governor, 3 or 4 foundation governors, 1 co-opted governor.

G   *Voluntary Controlled Primary School under 100 pupils* May choose between F and G. 3 parent governors, 2 LEA governors, 1 teacher governor, 1 or 0 staff governor, 2 foundation governors, 1 co-opted governor.

H   *Voluntary Aided Primary School* 1 or 2 parent governors, 1 or 2 LEA governors, 1 teacher governor, 1 staff governor, sufficient foundation governors to give a majority of two overall, and two of these at least must be parents.

I   *Voluntary Aided Primary School* under 100 pupils May choose between H and I. 1 parent governor, 1 LEA governor, 1 teacher governor, 1 or 0 staff governor, foundation governors as in H.

SECONDARY SCHOOLS

J   *Community Secondary School* 6 parent governors, 5 LEA governors, 2 teacher governors, 1 staff governor, 5 co-opted governors.

K   *Community Secondary School under 600 pupils* May choose between J and K. 5 parent governors, 4 LEA governors, 2 teacher governors, 1 staff governor, 4 co-opted governors

L   *Foundation Secondary School* 7 parent governors, 2 LEA governors, 2 teacher governors, 1 staff governor, 5 foundation governors, 3 co-opted governors.

M   *Foundation Secondary School under 600 pupils* May choose between L and M. 6 parent governors, 2 LEA governors, 2 teacher governors, 1 staff governor, 4 foundation governors, 2 co-opted governors.

N   *Voluntary Controlled Secondary School* 6 parent governors, 4 LEA governors, 2 teacher governors, 1 staff governor, 5 foundation governors, 3 co-opted governors.

O   *Voluntary Controlled Secondary School under 600 pupils* May choose between N and O. 5 parent governors, 3 LEA governors, 2 teacher governors, 1 staff governor, 4 foundation governors, 2 co-opted governors.

P   *Voluntary Aided Secondary School* 3 parent governors, 2 LEA governors, 2 teacher governors, 1 staff governor, sufficient foundation governors to give an overall majority of 3. Three of these must be parents.

Q   *Voluntary Aided Secondary School under 600 pupils* May choose between P and Q. 2 parent governors, 1 LEA governor, 2 teacher governors, 1 staff governor, sufficient foundation governors to give an overall majority of 2. Two of these must be parents.

Where in any category there is a choice of numbers for more than one kind of governor, e.g. in voluntary aided primary schools one or two parent governors and one or two LEA governors, a governing body must choose the higher or lower option wholesale, i.e. no mixing and matching.

Also by Joan Sallis

Managing Better With Governors:
A practical guide to working together for school success

Published by Financial Times Management in April 1999

This training manual, written by this country's most experienced writer, speaker and consultant on school governor issues, is a practical step-by-step companion for the head or would-be head who wants not just to 'manage' but to excel in this dimension of the school's work. Joan Sallis has worked with thousands of heads and deputies and written many best-selling guides, and for eleven years she has been 'agony aunt' to hundreds of heads and governors through the TES Agenda column. She is realistic about the difficulties and writes with warmth and sympathy, but the hard centre of this manual is a recognition that governors are here to stay, that their role is legitimate, and that a good relationship with the governing body is not only a positive strength to a school but a mark of the five star head.

The manual is designed for inter-active learning within and between schools and contains a large number of discussion papers, model processes and documents, and case studies, planned to support the appropriate subject sections.
These include:

- motivation
- expectations
- roles and respect for boundaries
- how to recruit and retain good governors
- team-building
- managing the work
- involving governors in school improvement

Perhaps the manual's most welcome section will be a guide to the nuts and bolts of sharing strategic school thinking with governors, **in step** rather than **in turns**, thus avoiding one of the head's most exhausting and unsatisfying experiences - having to do everything twice. An unusual feature for a management manual is the inclusion of ten parallel self-contained guides for governors, each related to a subject section, which head teachers can give to their governing bodies or use in discussion with them. These are designed to overcome the most common misunderstandings and dysfunctions of governing bodies and to direct their energies to the appropriate level of intervention. They draw on the author's wide experience.
Head teachers, those seeking headships, senior managers and governors will all find invaluable information and guidance in this manual. Purchasing schools may make up to ten photo-copies of working papers for their own use.

Price £69.00 + P & P £6.95

If you have found this book helpful you will be interested in...

... THE EFFECTIVE SCHOOL GOVERNOR

by David Marriott

£15.95

David Marriott is Head of Governor Support for Wiltshire. In this role he works closely with school governing bodies.

In **The Effective School Governor** David draws on his extensive experience and knowledge to provide an invaluable guide for new and experienced governors in both the primary and secondary phases.

He gives advice on how to be clear about personal strengths and how to make the most of them as a governor. He provides clear and practical guidance about working with others and succinctly sums up current thinking on how governors can perform effectively.

Included with the book is a free audio tape which allows busy governors to listen to the text at home or when on the move.

To order contact:

Network Educational Press Ltd, PO Box 635, Stafford, ST16 1BF
Tel 01785 225515
Fax 01785 228566
Website http: www.networkpress.co.uk
Email: enquiries@networkpress.co.uk

Other books from NEP

The NEP list includes a range of successful and well-received titles about the topics of more effective teaching and learning and school management. They also include books about many of the current issues faced by teachers, governors, advisers and inspectors at all levels and phases.

Teaching and Learning

Accelerated Learning in the Classroom Alistair Smith	£15.95
Accelerated Learning in Practice Alistair Smith	£19.95
The alps approach *(Accelerated Learning in the Primary School)* Alistair Smith	£17.95
Mapwise Oliver Caviglioli & Ian Harris *(available May 2000)*	£ 14.95
Effective Learning Activities Chris Dickinson	£10.95
Lessons are for Learning Mike Hughes	£12.95
Effective Learning in Science Keith Bishop & Paul Denley	£11.95
Closing the Learning Gap Mike Hughes	£15.95
Imagine That Steve Bowkett	£19.95
Self-intelligence Steve Bowkett	£19.95
Multiple Intelligence Posters	£23.44

School Management

The Well Teacher (available, March 2000) Maureen Cooper	£8.95
Managing Challenging People (available March 2000) Bev Curtis & Maureen Cooper	£8.95
Improving Personal Effectiveness for Managers in Schools James Johnson	£12.95
Effective Heads of Department Phil Jones & Nick Sparks	£10.95
Making Pupil Data Powerful Maggie Pringle & Tony Cobb	£12.95

Issues in Education

Raising Boys' Achievement   Jon Pickering   £12.95

**Effective Provision for Able
and Talented Children**   Barry Teare   £12.95

**Effective Resources for Able
and Talented Children**   Barry Teare   £12.95

Effective Careers Education & Guidance
Andrew Edwards & Anthony Barnes   £11.95

Best Behaviour
(plus free Best Behaviour FIRST AID)   Peter Relf et alia   £12.95

Helping with Reading   Angela White & Anne Butterworth   £14.95

Getting Started (for NQTs)   Henry Liebling   £12.95

Network Educational Press Ltd
PO Box 635, Stafford, ST16 1BF
Tel 01785 225515
Fax 01785 228566
Website URL: www.networkpress.co.uk
Email: enquiries@networkpress.co.uk

9 781855 390126